this must be the place

this must be the place

FOLLOWING THE BREADCRUMBS OF YOUR
PAST TO DISCOVER YOUR PURPOSE TODAY

JAMI NATO

BETHANYHOUSE

a division of Baker Publishing Group
Minneapolis, Minnesota

© 2023 by Jami Nato, LLC

Published by Bethany House Publishers
Minneapolis, Minnesota
www.bethanyhouse.com

Bethany House Publishers is a division of
Baker Publishing Group, Grand Rapids, Michigan

Printed in the United States of America

Library of Congress Cataloging-in-Publication Data
Names: Nato, Jami, author.
Title: This must be the place : following the breadcrumbs of your past to discover your purpose today / Jami Nato.
Description: Minneapolis, Minnesota : Bethany House Publishers, a division of Baker Publishing Group, [2023]
Identifiers: LCCN 2022049813 | ISBN 9780764241260 | ISBN 9781493442225 (ebook)
Subjects: LCSH: Christian life. | Conduct of life. | Self-consciousness (Awareness)
Classification: LCC BV4501.3 .N388 2023 | DDC 248.4–dc23/eng/20230126
LC record available at https://lccn.loc.gov/2022049813

The author is represented by To the Point Editorial Services.

Baker Publishing Group publications use paper produced from sustainable forestry practices and post-consumer waste whenever possible.

23 24 25 26 27 28 29   8 7 6 5 4 3 2

To my children: I had you in mind when I wrote this book.
I hope it helps you most of all when you feel
that you've lost your way.

Contents

Contents

I Saved a Seat for You

Have you ever experienced a Southwest flight? There are all these unspoken rules, people hogging the armrests, and the tiers of importance: groups A, B, or the dreaded C! And don't get me started on finding a place for your luggage in the back of the plane, then trying to walk against the sea of travelers in the wrong direction. I'm sweating just thinking about it.

Once when I was pregnant and had to put my luggage in the overhead bin, it felt like it took me three hours to finally find a spot. And because people magically lose their manners in airports (see also Costco), no one remembered they had hands to help this very pregnant woman. The worst part was that I did finally get my suitcase up into a bin, but it didn't quite fit. So as I was trying to rearrange someone else's luggage as if I were playing a sweaty game of *Tetris*, I hit the guy below me on the head with two very swift tummy taps. Right on the head. I was mortified but also pleased that my baby helped me knock some sense into the passenger who eventually got up. *Oh, you needed help?*

Life can feel like a bad flight sometimes. You may feel like a C passenger struggling to find a place for your suitcase while no one notices. But with God's seating arrangements, there's no rush or hustle to find your seat. There's no wondering where you're supposed to sit or unspoken rules or questioning whether you're annoying your seatmate. He's already tagged a specific seat for you, and while you're on the same plane, you're most certainly on a different journey than the person next to you.

Your journey may not look like you had hoped it would. You may have what feels like too many layovers, a few detours, and frustrating delays. But every experience, good or bad, molds and contours who we are today and directs us toward who and what we are meant to be. I truly believe these experiences are hand-tailored to highlight the gifts God has already appointed in each of us and to give a unique empathy to each of us. When you pair a unique empathy with a unique gifting, you find your calling. (I'll help you discover this in the coming chapters, and I promise you it will be more fun than painful.) And that unique calling is not to build up our kingdoms but to go and build his by simply being exactly who he made us to be, not who he made others to be.

> Each of you should use whatever gift you have received to serve others, as faithful stewards of God's grace in its various forms. If anyone speaks, they should do so as one who speaks the very words of God. If anyone serves, they should do so with the strength God provides, so that in all things God may be praised through Jesus Christ. To him be the glory and the power for ever and ever. Amen.
>
> 1 Peter 4:10–11 NIV

It's like God has given each of his children a treasure map. While the destination is the same, the routes are as unique as we are. We are trying to get from the start to the big X that marks treasure, bringing his kingdom to earth in our unique way. But it's never a straight line, is it? There are obstacles and comic relief. There are beautiful and weird and even seemingly dangerous things. It feels dangerous to ask questions about our faith and about God. Maybe it feels like you're doubting him and, thus, somehow sinning—as if he can't handle your questions about himself and you and your purpose in life. It can feel dangerous to be curious if all you've known in life is the very comfortable idol of control (ask me how I know!). And no one really wants to look at suffering, to look back. We think we're going to be turned into a pillar of salt for it (didn't that Bible story scare the knock-off Marshmallow Mateys cereal out of you?). The truth is that revisiting suffering to find meaning is something we are challenged to do as we recount the suffering of God's people over and over in the Bible. He gave us so many specific stories to help us see him more clearly, to ask where he was and who he is during the pain.

A straight line wouldn't allow us to see our need for God's mercy and his tender guidance as we brave our tenuous journey. Each place, each stop on the way is necessary and never wasted. I'll give you lots of examples so you won't have to do this alone.

God left us breadcrumbs along the way because he knew we would get lost. Those breadcrumbs are the things you are naturally good at, skills you've learned, and weird things that make you YOU: the suffering, the obstacles, the experiences, the relationships, the joys, and the mundane. I want you to see those things as a way to transform those you influence, those who are right in front of you. Many of us believe a false narrative in which we have to have a big audience to make a real impact. The truth is that Jesus taught that every single person we encounter is important. Perhaps it's your children. Perhaps it's your neighborhood or the elementary school where you volunteer. Maybe you're an entrepreneur with five employees or a CEO with five hundred. Maybe it's a friend group, a college sorority, your knitting-with-cat-hair group. With God, nothing is wasted; every single situation is on purpose. If we believed that, we would see our lives differently. We would start paying attention to each detail and looking back for the breadcrumbs that have been there all along.

We don't know where our faithfulness will end up; we only know that God asks us to be faithful to his calling on our lives right on the path he's mapped for us.

The first time I spoke about breadcrumbs to a large audience, my goal was to give those forty thousand listeners in the audience a new pair of glasses. (Pro tip: If you imagine everyone naked and wearing glasses, it will make you MORE nervous, not less.) So I did every-thing I could to get their attention (you know, dance, wear armpit pads, mess up my PowerPoint—the usual speaker stuff) and show what I was good at—selling an idea—and not so good at—following the rules. I was not going to let them leave that auditorium without knowing that everything and anything could be used for their good if they had a new perspective.

Let me show you what my treasure map looks like, where I got lost along the way, and how the breadcrumbs helped me find my way. Then I'll guide you to do some reflective work to make sense of your own treasure map. You'll have to look back. You'll have to look forward. You'll have to do some digging and get a little dirty—wait, are we about to discover the next hidden city or a cluster of dinosaur bones? My inner six-year-old is excited about this! You'll even have to pay attention to some things you've long ignored. But what you'll discover will confirm who you are and who you are meant to be. Keep in mind that my map won't look like yours—and it shouldn't. My big-gest hope is that you gain so much confidence in what God has done in your life and where he's taking you that you change your family, school, neighborhood, city, and the world for the Gospel of Christ!*

The stories from my life will be the flashlight to shine on the breadcrumbs that God has left for you on all parts of your journey:

- Where you've been (part 1)
- Where you are (part 2)
- Where you want to go (part 3)

My goal is to help you realize that nothing is wasted. Where you are today is the very place you're supposed to be . . . in fact, *This Must Be the Place.*

....

* I hope you're slow clapping at this point because I yelled that last sentence!

Following Your Breadcrumbs

If you're like me, chances are that you've found your identity in many roles outside of God's child. I remember when I got the results from a genetics test that told me all sorts of quirky things, one being that I was built as a "power athlete." Go ahead and laugh (my friends who are true athletes sure do!), but I did always wonder why I could catch a diaper thrown across the room easily, or why I could beat everyone at cornhole without any practice. (TRY ME . . . I will crush you!) Growing up, though, I was told I wasn't good at sports because I was super short, didn't have the money to start sports early, and had a hard time paying attention. So I stopped trying and started believing I'm no good. My genetics say otherwise! Sometimes that's how we walk around too. God says we are made uniquely and wildly loved and accepted, but we walk around wondering who we are and if we have a place at the table.

Can you list all the labels placed on you in your life (Intentional Mother, Good Wife, Mediocre Sister, World's Okayest Friend, Thoughtful Neighbor, Best Jazzerciser) to see the areas where you've found approval, accolades, or even hurtful mislabels?

Which one most defines who you are and why? Which ones remind you of your identity in Christ and which ones pull you away from that? Ask God to meet you in these places and transform how you see yourself so your view takes on his lens.

PART 1

Where You've Been

one

My First Kickstarter

Really, if you want to know who funded my first Kickstarter campaign, it was Mrs. Yollands (that's *Yawllllands* with a thick Texas accent), who lived catty-corner from our pink house on Monroe Street. She wore a green, belted jumpsuit and had short white hair. Her house smelled like stale smoke, mothballs, canned soup, and hairspray. Perhaps she was lonely, because she always let me come inside to peddle my worn plastic sack of rocks.

I would plop down on her itchy, blue floral chair and the smoke would exude from the cushion like I was the character Pigpen on *Peanuts*. It would have been endearing, except I had terrible allergies, so my eyes puffed up, and I sneezed aggressively. I would talk with her for hours and hours. Well, probably more like ten minutes, but those minutes were very long. The only thing that kept me in that chair was the yellow candy dish full of Red Hots and the thrill of a sale I was about to make. While she told me stories about her dog (which I'm not sure was alive), I zoned out and studied her glass hutch full of porcelain cat treasures. As a matter of fact, she told me the same dog stories over and over and never remembered my name, just that I was one of the many offspring from across the street. In hindsight, she

17

might have had some dementia—which is probably why I kept selling her rocks from her own yard and she kept buying them. For what it's worth, I did pick the prettiest ones. Sometimes people just need you to curate what's right in front of their faces so they see the value. Even if, as a safety precaution, you should not have gone into her house and should have reported to your parents that the dog never moved.

As the seasons progressed, I also sold seeds to her and a couple other neighbors. Zinnia seeds from Mr. Baggott's backyard, four houses down. He was a hermit who never came out of his house. We would peek into the windows to see if we could catch a glimpse of the myth and the legend, but I never saw him. His yard was ripe with business "opportunity." I wonder why he didn't yell at us to stop picking the black seeds off the stems. He certainly couldn't have enjoyed the muddy mess we tracked through his yard, bringing it into our yard and eventually landing it in our house, throwing Mother into a tantrum. I think this was why my mother, with a baby on her hip, locked the doors and threw sandwiches to us out the side window and onto the trampoline. "Have a picnic!" she'd yell. And we were thrilled.

My mother had six children at the time (more would come later), four of which were in diapers, and was often in a blur of exhaustion. So we played outside for hours and hours without coming home until dark. Not that I gave her much consideration, I just knew she was always inside cooking beans or changing diapers or cleaning up some mess. Mom was both intensely familiar and deeply mysterious to me as a child. She could have been knitting sweaters made of cat hair or making a spaceship so she could escape our small town for all I knew.*

....

* I would sometimes run into the bathroom and see toilet paper with black smudges on it in the toilet. How strange that Mother has black boogers. Confused, I wondered how it got there—I tried to solve the riddle off and on for years. After throwing my own mascara-laden tissue in the toilet during my first year of motherhood, it hit me. Like me, she was crying; she was tired of making ends meet, and I, in the joys of childhood, had no idea how tight things were.

I had plenty of freedom to do mostly whatever I wanted, within reason. While other children wrestled on the trampoline or played hide and seek, I was on a mission of hustling for a goal. At the corner store was a glass case of all things random—jewelry, baseball cards, and the shining Mecca of all my ten-year-old dreams: New Kids on the Block trading cards. Oh, the glory of Jonathan, Joey, Jordan, Danny, and Donnie! I had listened to them in my room on the brown shag carpet for hours, lying close to the speakers, staring at the popcorn ceiling, and memorizing the words.

Obviously if they knew me—poor, stringy haired, garage-sale-clothes-wearing, rock-selling gal—they would want to spend time with me. What a catch. But as I couldn't afford to go to a concert, nor would my mother allow me to go see anyone else but Amy Grant, the trading cards would suffice. (In truth, my parents also let me see The Power Team. How was I not scarred for life when they lay on a bed of nails and someone hammered a cinder block on their chests "for the Lord"?) The thing about collections is that they're never ending; you always need more. And the thing about being poor is that your parents never give you money and you never ask for it anyway because it isn't there. So each week, I set out to earn more and more by swindling all my neighbors. I would need two dollars each week or so to get a new set of five cards, and there were four sets, so if you do the math—I would need like $800,000 in cash.

So that's where you would find me: building relationships living room to living room. First with Mrs. Yollands, then over to Melba, who was hard of hearing, then with Caroline next door. Caroline was always good for a pity sale even though she already had a garden full of rocks and zinnias. She knew I was hustling so, when her family went out of town for the weekend, she asked me to watch their bird. I was thrilled to have another stream of income and gladly accepted.

The problem was that I also had a beloved cat that followed me as I went door to door. Truth be told, I don't know why the cat and I made fast friends, but we had a strong connection after another family decided to give her away on account of allergies. I also had terrible allergies and a nose full of snot to prove it. The cat was brindled and silky and moody, and her name was Dollface. Coincidentally, she was not anything like a doll. That's probably why she was given away.

This cat was more like a gangster walking the streets on the prowl. Aside from following me around, she was very independent, very scrappy. Once I watched her get hit by a car. She jumped up and ran up a tree with blood coming from her nose. I yelled for my mother to call 911 while I sat below the tree. Tears running down my face, I hollered for Dollface to come down. She wouldn't. Sweating, hair matted to my face, I wondered if she had died up there and why the fire department never came. Later in the cool of the day, she climbed down the giant tree and came home with me. When I walked in the door, my mother exclaimed, "That cat will never die!" And that is true; my love kept that cat alive for too long. She stayed with me through a lot of heartache as a child and a lot of fearful nights.

To me, she was a sweet animal fixture on my chest while I slept who continued to lovingly give me terrible allergies that we didn't have medicine to fix. In the morning she would lick my eyes open and gently pat my face to wake me (even though she had claws). I knocked food off the table "accidentally" for her and snuck milk for her at night. When I was seven or so, with a very creative imagination, I pretended to be a cat with her for about a year and wouldn't break character. To the point where I napped on the porch and drank water from a bowl that my mother set down with an eye roll and a sigh. I loved when the mailman stepped over me while I was catnapping. I would meow at him as he placed the mail in the door slot, to which he would reply, "Oh, my. They must have gotten a new cat!"

What I'm getting at is that while I was lost in the imaginary cat world, Dollface was an actual cat who liked to eat mice and apparently also birds. She followed me to Caroline's house where I was bird-sitting, saw a delicious prize, somehow opened the cage (that I probably didn't shut), and promptly ate the bird, leaving a wing and some feathers for show when I went to check on it that night. Through tears I came up with a plan to break the news to my neighbors with a gentle buffer: I would forgo the New Kids on the Block trading cards and, instead, buy a new bird. I simply had to sell more seeds, hustle harder, and never again agree to watch something my cat would eat. It was a small setback in my summer goals. I gathered all the neighbor kids and told them the vision: we needed to collect more seeds and expand the territory to the next block to get a new bird . . . even though it was my fault and they had no skin in the game.

Despite the setbacks, I did end up making enough money to buy all of the trading cards that summer. The saddest part of the whole deal was that in a moment of distraction, I laid the cards on our 1980s hand-me-down waterbed. My brothers jumped on the bed, and gentle vinyl waves pushed the cards to the sides, lodging them into the crevices. I came back and swore I had set them right there! Naturally, for weeks I blamed my brothers for stealing my collection. That is, until the bed sprung a leak and deflated (oh, the perils of sleeping on water!). We found the cards soaked and mangled as we threw the giant bed in dumpster hell where it belonged, along with the moldy New Kids on the Block. Two huge losses in one day: one in size, the other in the form of my hard-earned money.

While this story isn't a real heartwarmer of triumph, it was the first time I had a goal and accomplished something without the help of my parents. I made something out of nothing, and I was proud of it. There was something special about earning money outside of a chore. I learned money doesn't always come from parents, birthdays, or the luck of a dime on the sidewalk. My gift was the joy of the neighborhood hustle, building relationships, and selling. And it was one obscure woman across a brick roadway on Monroe Street who kept buying my rocks. Long gone as she is, her voice still talks to the little girl living inside of me: "Come in. Tell me more! How much for that one?"

For many years, I had often thought what a strange kid I was. But there came a time in my career when I wondered why I loved selling stuff so much. What was the thrill of it? Why am I like this? Did God make people to sell? I could make a video about a spray cleaner set to a medley of gangster rap while I shuffled with delicious mom moves across the kitchen go viral. I could motivate a room full of women by telling vulnerable stories about myself and how God still loves me and still chooses to use me. I felt guilty for enjoying my career in sales and leadership. It's just not what women do. Especially good Christian women. But God didn't make me like this on accident. I was not defective material that somehow didn't get the right wiring. Accepting and embracing my real identity frees me to let God do work in others and in me. If I don't have to be the Holy Spirit for you, that frees me up to focus on my own work with the Lord. I can stop judging everyone else. How freeing to look at where God is leading me and has been leading me.

We're about to go on one of those terrifying, but fun, twisty-turny water park slides, so I hope you'll join me as we look at where God has been in your past, where he's with you today, and where you're going as you dream for the future.

> *When I look back, I see that God was leaving breadcrumbs for me: "I made you to do this! Run with it!"*

When I look back, I see that God was leaving breadcrumbs for me: "I made you to do this! Run with it!" Since I stopped fighting it, there has been such joy in living in my design, running freely in the gifts my good Father gave just for me. By the way, I have a few really sparkly rocks in my front yard if you'd like to get first dibs!

· · · · · · · · · · **Following Your Breadcrumbs** · · · · · · · · · ·

Too many of us question our gifts and our longings. It may be because we've been told they don't fit in the proper mold, or someone thinks we should be different, or we've been wanting others' gifts for so long that we've forgotten how to see worth in our own. Let me explain.

My husband is as blind as a bat. I remember trying to get a prescription for him at Costco, and they had to refer him to a specialist. That's how bad his eyes were! Several years into our marriage, his parents gave him Lasik surgery for a birthday present. After the surgery, I was amazed. I was used to him not seeing so clearly. One morning, he was looking at me lovingly—I thought. But it turned out he had found a really wiry chin hair. "Wow, babe! We both have beards!" We died laughing.

When he could finally see properly, he noticed so many more details that he had never seen clearly before.

That's what I'm here to do for you: give you a new pair of glasses to put on. When I have eternal glasses on, I am quick to see everything in my life more clearly. I don't take on false identities that hinder me from doing the work I am made to do here on this earth. I can immediately see where I've been distracted from my true purpose and gotten off track. I can see the very specific events in my life that God has used to shape me. I can see the path behind me and the way ahead. It's time to reorient your thinking and reassess the value of what you have diminished for far too long.

Look back to when you were about eight to ten years old because that's when you were likely your truest self and showed pure intentions. I may have been selling rocks, but you may have been painting, teaching the neighbor kids, or operating on your stuffed animals or siblings. Maybe you were on adventures by the creek or collecting frogs and spiders. Whatever you were doing then holds clues for today. Maybe it is in rocks and seeds, free to everyone else. But everyone else, even children, are pursuing what God made them to do, too, if you simply watch. Watch them with delight: the performers, the builders, the lemonade stands, the fashion shows, the sword wielders.

My treasure map word:
ENTREPRENEUR

When you were a child, what did you spend time on and really enjoy?

Do you still spend time on any of those things as an adult?

two

Surprise!

People on welfare in the 1980s received enough "government cheese" to quite literally put it on everything. Did my mom go to the grocery store with food stamps for it, or was there an official government cheese office where someone handed irregularly long, orange rectangles through a hole in the glass? Like a train ticket, but the destination is high cholesterol and constipation. All I know is that cheese allotment corresponded to family size. In our case, this was ten people, two reproducing Chow Chows, and one cat that would never die. If you're wondering, yes, pets can eat orange cheese and live longer than they should.

When I first got married, I thought a good meal was slow-cooked pinto beans, salted and then sprinkled with orange cheese, served with off-brand saltine crackers. I remember my new husband sitting there with a side smile, trying to be grateful. To me, it tasted like the magic of childhood. To him, it tasted like, well, plain ol' beans with orange highlights.* From then on, I learned to add meat and

---

* Nothing amplifies the differences in two people's upbringings than that first awkward year in marriage. I didn't understand until then why marriage books kept saying, "Marriage is a mirror." It's like all the things we didn't see before, we now see: the wiry chin hairs, the booger no one told you about all through lunch, or the aggressive overuse of cheddar cheese.

turn it into what the middle class call *chili*, but it took me a while to toot my way into that sort of change.

I still can't help but look at the ways growing up poor shaped me. It colored the way I see the world. It used to annoy me, and I felt a little ashamed, but now I see it as an asset. For instance, some of my favorite things that came straight from growing up poor and bring me so much joy are free items, bargains, coupons, bang-and-dent items, and garage sales. Who even needs real stores when you can spend your time haggling a stranger over one whole dollar? When we first got married, I would call my husband and say things like, "I found this couch two streets over on the curb." He would go begrudgingly to pick up a delicious, burnt orange couch from Buena Vista Street—which served us for five years. Did I think about bed bugs? No. Same with the wooden coffee table we snagged on big-trash pickup day. Repainted, it was a beaut—until our oldest jumped off it and broke the legs—but hey, it was free.99. I loved the sense of being resourceful and creative, skills that helped me turn nothing into something. I loved using what I had and multiplying it. I'm not saying I'm Jesus turning two loaves and five fish into a dinner for five thousand, but maybe it's an eternal trait.

Our home was practically furnished in others' trash and floor model sales (those were considered a major splurge). We used our wedding gift cards to buy a crib nine months after our honeymoon (that happened a little quicker than planned). We were happy and scrappy, making our own way, even if our house looked only slightly more sanitary than a college frat living room.

We didn't have much, but we were making it work.

Growing up, I watched my mother hit garage sales for all our clothes and toys. As you can guess, clothing eight kids was no easy task on a very limited budget. But we were always happy when she unloaded the car with a smile. *Did she find anything for me?* She would be out all day, in the rain or heat, her dedication unmatched. I remember the paper being laid out on the table the night before with garage sale ads circled. We have it so easy now with online shopping, Facebook Marketplace, and GPS, but that's why everyone is so soft. You don't know what it feels like to show up at a stranger's house, who could be a serial killer, after you got lost four times—and then to leave with twenty-two items you weren't even shopping for (but that the Lord obviously provided). THE THRILL!

Mom would leave with her best friends no later than 7:45 a.m. and sometimes, if I was up and promised not to whine, she'd let me come along. As I got older, I learned that waking up early on Friday was to my advantage. I could immediately veto that brown corduroy jumper with the coordinating turtleneck so I wouldn't be forced to itch my way through church next Sunday. But I also learned how to search for treasure in the midst of junk, to see something others might not see. I learned how important the hunt was, the time it took to prepare, the joy of finding the perfect item—and how to graciously peruse a garage while holding your breath and feigning interest while the only thing you leave with is a mold allergy. I remember the small talk, the stories, the one-on-one time with my mom. Radio blaring in the old, yellow van with brown shag carpet interior, hot summer days with the windows down, and the vinyl seats sticking to our legs so hard we lost three layers of skin when we got up too fast. The world was ours, and we were conquering it one bargain at a time.

As my parents' means increased, I wondered why my mom would still stop at garage sales, boasting of her finds at dinner. "Can you believe it? This brand-new bed-in-a-bag set for ten dollars, Jami!" I never thought I needed a leopard bedspread with leopard pillows and leopard window coverings. But that day, the Lord answered a prayer I hadn't even thought to ask. I had that bed set for longer than I should have, but you don't slap the goodness of the Father's animal-print hand away. No, you receive it with gratitude and go to the wallpaper store to find a luxurious border to match it.

The other day while I was clipping a coupon, my husband looked at me and said, "You know, you could just go buy that." And I threw the scissors at him. Just kidding, but I did throw a dagger with my words.

"You can't take the poor girl out of me!" I do sometimes resent her when I don't think there will be enough for me and collect and hoard *just in case*. And while I sometimes do fall into the trap of *more will make me happy*, for the most part, I enjoy the grateful, resourceful woman God created through my childhood. Growing up with nothing was not for nothing. We had something; it just wasn't in the nicest things or tangible possessions. We had hard work and resourcefulness.

I find the greatest delight in someone else's trash becoming a treasure. I love seeing beyond the messed-up piece of furniture and painting it in my head, then giving it a new life with a little elbow grease. I'm not afraid to work to uncover the potential. It makes a piece all the more meaningful to know God provided for me while fostering a gift I would need later on in life. Yes, he gave me a free, worn-out coffee table and a million other items to outfit our first home. Even now, that memory brings a smile to my face. But learning to be faithful with the process of needing, finding, and restoring was teaching me to be faithful with little so that one day, I would have the skills to be faithful with what's big.

Our first house was less than one thousand square feet. The location was great, but the house and the street not so much. We learned how to do everything ourselves (as much as we could) to make it better. We painted everything, tiled everything (please ignore the sloppy grout lines), finished the basement, doubled the square footage, and loved the heck out of it. In that house we had two babies, created lots of memories, and experienced some suffering we would gladly leave behind. So we sold it and turned a good profit.

I laugh because I found the new house on Craigslist and fell in love with the gray saltbox colonial and its potential. We didn't have a realtor, and the sellers didn't either. While I don't recommend that, it helped us jump into a new neighborhood we probably had no business being in. We snuck in the back door. The vision was there: *Wouldn't this house look great with three dormers? We could build out the attic space. Now because we're gluttons for punishment, let's also live through a kitchen renovation.* Little by little, we made that gray colonial shine.* I posted pictures on my blog and somehow it landed us in a magazine. Pinterest went wild with it, and suddenly I had a following, as haphazard as it felt. But God was clearly leading us.

Just as we had finished those projects, an opportunity came along to help plant a church at the same time we were looking for a school for our differently abled kiddo. We had worked so hard on our house with no intention of selling but felt like we needed to be obedient in what God was asking us to do. So we decided to make the *dreaded* move to the suburbs that we had judged others for making. We began looking for a house in the school district our daughter needed and closer to the new church where God was leading us. We found a house that was in dire need of updating and at the top of our price range. When I walked into the house six hundred months pregnant, I said a big fat NO. The outside was beautiful, but it would be too much work.

That night, in my head, I started painting the walls and ripping out the carpet. Of course, the beams could stay. I added new subway tile on the backsplash, scraped the popcorn ceilings, and rearranged our furniture. *Dang it! Why are you giving me a vision for this, Lord? You know we can't afford this house.* In the morning, after much prayer, I told my husband I was okay moving forward with an offer. While he was thrilled, I was petrified. I just didn't know if I had what it would take for this magnitude of a project on a smallish budget, and yet I said something then that I still say now as a mantra when I'm walking in obedience but afraid of failing: "He's done it before, and he'll do it again." My confidence *in myself* shifted immediately to my confidence *in him*, and I became instantly light.

....

* In that charming neighborhood, we learned how to hire pros for projects we weren't trained to even think about doing.

We secured the house, and I leaned on my past ten years of being faithful with what was small and on ten-year-old me who loved finding treasure, having a vision for something others might call trash, and redeeming it. Through a lot of ups and downs, including having to urgently borrow money from my parents (0/5 stars, do not recommend), the house was ready for the baby to arrive a couple of weeks later. *Phew!* We didn't know what we were doing, but we kept taking giant faith leaps forward, trusting that God knew where we were going all along.

> *"He's done it before, and he'll do it again." My confidence in myself shifted immediately to my confidence in him, and I became instantly light.*

By now, you won't be surprised to learn that three years ago, we decided to look for a flip house to work on, not to live in. As we began looking, I loved lots of houses, and we even made offers on a few that fell through. I was disappointed. "Will we ever find something?!" I grew a little frustrated and sort of gave up on finding anything that fit the criteria we thought we wanted.

WE thought WE wanted.

A little while later, my husband went to lunch with a buddy who mentioned his wife was trying to sell a lake house that had been on the market for five years. It had been through four realtors; she was the last. The price had been dropping and dropping, and my husband had always dreamed of owning a lake house, so we decided to take a look. I did this begrudgingly and with a bad attitude, as I am not a huge fan of lakes—or what I call "poop water." No input and no output, to me, says bacterial infection. I couldn't believe people actually desired to live on this body of water.*

When we walked in, I tried to be a good sport. My husband seemed to love it, and I kept thinking, *Um, no. We can't afford this*

---

* As you can see, my opinions were strong and possibly rude.

30

and it needs so much work and what about the plan to flip some-thing? This didn't fit what we thought we wanted. Then I saw the view. I didn't want to admit it, but my heart was pinged. *Nope, not today, Satan . . . we're going to stay the course.* My course, of course. I told the realtor it was a no for me, and my husband kind of pouted. On the way home, I explained how unrealistic it would be. He sighed, sort of agreeing.

That night as I lay in bed trying to fall asleep, I began build-ing a bunk room on the empty top floor. I ripped up the bright navy carpet and added wood floors and pretty rugs. I painted the kitchen cabinets and added new countertops. I pictured us on a boat. *NOOOOOOOO! It's happening again!* "Lord, this is impos-sible. Why are you doing this?" I asked. The next day, my husband met with our financial adviser, who said we could take equity out of our house to put into the lake house. It was like God had made us a secret savings account we didn't even think about. I couldn't believe it.

As we made plans to renovate this mammoth of a house, we had a vision of having retreats there and hosting lots of people. We would need a nice kitchen and a lot of places to sleep, so kitchen and bunk room it was. Everything else could wait. We held that vision along the tedious journey of designing, dealing with contractors, decorat-ing, and almost losing our sanity. In the end, our clearance buy with a great view turned into Cinderella at the ball.

When my mother said she and my dad wanted to come over to pray for my new property venture, she had a specific word for us. I thought, *Well, can't say no to the Lord.** As she oohed and aahed at the house, she said with a smile, "I think God specifically said the word *surprise* when I was praying over this house."

....

* You may not have grown up in a charismatic church environment, but if you did, you understand that if someone says, "I have a word for you," you immediately start praying for an interpretation and grab your shofar on the way to meet them.

Nato* and I laughed. "Like SURPRISE! You guys are idiots? Or surprise, this is good? Or what is going to happen?" She wasn't sure. It was tempting to think of the worst, to let my mind roam into thinking God was going to punish us for taking on a project too big with too much invested. This was so far beyond poor-girl treasures! But as my husband and I were talking that night, we had to remind each other of the truth about God's character: He is good, and he wants our good. And where God had shown up for us time and time again was in real estate ventures. He led us here, and we were obedient. "He has done this before, and he'll do it again."

Just as the house got its final touches weeks later, the COVID-19 pandemic hit. We were, in fact, watching the news from the lake house living room as I was ripping tags off pillows and blankets to make the bunk beds. We heard of a strange new virus making its way to the United States soon. Our dreams of hosting retreats quickly vanished between the morning and the afternoon. We canceled any gatherings, and the world grew eerily silent. Nowhere to go, nowhere to travel to. No sports events, no going to school, no eating out. *You must stay right where you are.*

Talk about a surprise. This wasn't working out at all like *we had planned.* What a huge interruption to the dreams we thought God had given us. But that year, we lived in the oasis we intended for others to find rest in. We had been running so hard creating a space for others, we didn't even consider that perhaps we were creating a soft place to land for ourselves.

Did I mention the address was C19?

---

* When I met Mark, everyone at the youth group where we worked together called him Nato, so I thought that was his first name. Or maybe I didn't think about it at all. I only figured out his name was "Mark" when I went to meet his parents two weeks into dating and his mother greeted him at the door with "Hello, Mark!" Oopsies. I've never stopped calling him Nato unless I'm super mad. If I use his first name, it probably means he's sleeping on the couch that night.

As we drove into the lake area every day to finish up loose ends and projects, knowing it would be more of a retreat for us that year, we had to continually drive by the local coffee shop on the corner. It kept catching my eye. It was rarely open, and when it was, the coffee was mediocre and the pastries didn't work for our gluten-free family. "Baby, that shop could be so great. The location is perfect, right? *Someone* should buy it and make it great. It could be so cute . . . they need to be using local coffee too."

He looked at me and said emphatically, "No, Jami Nato. Don't you even think about it."

But that night, in my head, I started putting shiplap on the walls and redoing the tile on the floor. *Uh-oh! Here we go again . . .*

Following Your Breadcrumbs

It's incredible to think that the place you grew up, with all the quirks, foibles, and beauty (or maybe your town was dry, mostly brown, and flat like mine) was a uniquely God-built experience for you. Like how tomatoes need a lot of heat and sun to be big, juicy tomatoes. Like Jami Nato needed to be fed a lot of government cheese to learn to be scrappy and resourceful so she could be the Jami Nato-est Jami that ever Jami-ed. You needed your specific environment too!

My treasure map word:
RESOURCEFUL

What experience from childhood, adolescence, or young adulthood has shaped you into who you are today? Maybe you grew up on a farm or deep in the city, maybe your grandparents raised you, maybe you grew up in a strict religious environment, maybe your kids experienced what I call a "Montessori parental experience" like mine (oh, I'm supposed to be the one in charge?).

How has that given you insight, helped you excel in a unique skill, or shaped your empathy?

Can you see where God was providing for you in some way, while fostering a passion for the future?

three

The End Is the Way

It's important for you to know that I'm writing this all in hindsight —thirteen years of hindsight. It's not like it never happened, but the distance I've had from the greatest heartache of my life has been kind to my heart and mind.

My plan was to be an A+ Christian lady who did really good work for God, and in turn, he would bless me and I wouldn't have to suffer all that much. I was an every-Sunday churchgoer and attended Bible studies. I brought meals to people in need and always set my Bible on the dash when I got pulled over for speeding. (I wasn't opposed to using God to get me out of a mess!) The unspoken agreement I signed said, "God Owes Me," but apparently he forgot his pen. So when my life fell apart, I was wholly unprepared. Maybe because I had a toddler and a newborn, and that's its own shitshow of exhaustion—with a lot of dirty diapers. I was bleary-eyed. My body was a weird carcass of expansion and deflation. My breasts were misshapen udders that suddenly stopped making milk the evening I read text messages from another woman to my husband.

They weren't garden variety texts like "How are you today, Good Lady?" More like "I can't stop thinking about what we did last night" and other salacious and devastating text bubbles. Even now, I sometimes have to tell myself not to think about those messages for fear I might throw a TV remote, rogue LEGO, or three to four unwashed steak knives at my husband. As I said, we have a lot of distance from this time in our marriage, but sometimes I still find myself angry about what he did.

He had a great new job after leaving the nursing profession and was moving into the land of medical device sales. We had bargained for a higher paycheck, and he got it! We were so thrilled about the new opportunities and how much easier it was to live without scrounging for quarters in the couch for Dairy Queen date nights. I was proud of him. We had worked so hard on his interview questions. He's not a quick responder; he likes to have the question, think about it for three days, and then answer thoughtfully. I, on the other hand, view life as one big improv stage. So I had come up with questions, and we had worked on stories of past work experiences. I drilled him with note cards for two weeks like it was the MCAT exam.

"That answer is too vague. You need to think of a time you showed you were a team player in the ICU. You can't just say you're a team player." Little did I know how much of a team player he was with one of his female coworkers. He opened up to her about struggles at home and in our marriage, and she comforted him. At first with words and affirmations, and then physically in a one-night stand.*

---

* I am still confused by this concept of a one-time giving of your body and soul over to someone: Does this happen accidentally? Or do you feed the bear every day in the driveway when you get home from work, and one Saturday, it shows up at your door? Then you invite it in and give it a collar and leash you've been making to keep it in check. But once inside, the bear is too powerful and snaps the leash. It chews up the couch, splits the down feather pillows, breaks all the dishes, leaves deep claw marks in the hardwood, and destroys family photos peppering the walls on the way out.
It's the latter.

He buried that experience and showed up to eat the dinner I had made him after he had been with her. He painstakingly tried to eat spaghetti with his stomach churning, knowing he had just finished dining at the table of broken vows. We carried on that year as if nothing had happened. Mainly because I didn't know anything had happened.

For him, the shame was heavy and, as anyone can imagine, crushing. There was only hiding in darkness, and without repentance, no light touched it. There was no power for supernatural change. Of course, like shame promises, there was behavioral change for a while, but a few years later, he found himself in another, deeper affair.*

There are a lot of things I want to clarify here because of what I had thought of others when they were getting a divorce:

I'm not an idiot.

We were having sex.

He still said he loved me every day.

We prayed together.

He helped with the dishes when he was home.

He still loved his kids.

I thought his new job was just taking a lot of time to get going.

We still went on dates.

Everything seemed okay. Until it wasn't. One autumn month, he turned a corner, and quickly our marriage took a nosedive. He had made a secret choice and turned his heart toward it. My husband became unrecognizable. It's difficult to explain the ways in which

---

* One of the things we believe now and teach our children is that true change comes from love, not from shame. We teach that with our whole hearts because we lived through the painful cycle of short-term shame-change and don't wish that roller coaster of self-hatred on anyone.

I felt unloved, the ways in which he ran into calamity, dragging me behind him.

I could tell you about the time I had just had our second baby and he kept trying to leave the hospital to "go back to work." While I was fresh with stitches after his child ripped through me, the sacrifice of my body still raw. I limped to the bathroom thinking, *This is not who he is.* I knew that because he had fallen in love with me when I had the flu and looked my worst and he had tenderly loved our first child and wouldn't dare leave his side or mine. My husband loved to help; he loved to rescue. And maybe that's what he was doing with this new woman: someone sick trying to rescue someone sick.

I could tell you about the year he wore a watch the first woman had given him and had said it was from his boss. "A Fossil watch? Is this the 90s? You don't even like Fossil." He wore it in our Christmas photos that year where we were holding our brand-new baby. Later that watch bragged, mocked, and heckled me in the hallway as I passed. They had bought gifts for each other, a brazen showcasing of a prize that would turn out to be shackles.

I could tell you about the New Year's Eve party when he left right before midnight because he had to "go into a trauma case," even calling his own pager to make it ping in front of everyone. Like Pavlov's dog, if I heard that signal of abandonment today, you would see me involuntarily wince, my shoulders would move to my ears, my breath caught in my chest like a prisoner.

I stood there crying in my friend's bedroom. I had to do the air flap thing with my hands to dry up my tears—which is as helpful as using a squirt gun for a forest fire, but I still had to pretend to maintain my dignity, even in a dark hour. My eyes were burning when I went out to the group to ask for a ride home. The home he would not come to that night. I sat in the driveway and told our friends something was wrong. They both believed me but had a hard time believing my husband—and their good friend—could be so offtrack. Our kids were at their grandparents' house that night, and I had been looking forward to reconnecting without all the noise. Which made walking in even lonelier at one in the morning.

Just get to the bed. I did not undress. I slid into the cold sheets and put my hand on his pillow, languishing. All while he was sleeping in someone else's tangled bedspread, fingers in someone else's hair, her arm on his chest. That night, I begged God through hot tears to get me out of this misery, whatever it was. (I still did not know about the affair.) *I think I might die. It's okay if I do, just peacefully in my sleep. I'd rather die than live one more day like this.* When the morning came, the door hinges announced his arrival. He was home, tiptoeing in. I pretended to be asleep as the shower began to run. Wash it all away.

I had a dream later that week. I say dream because if you say "vision," people tend to think you're a snake handler with a tambourine in one hand and a ribbon in the other. Regardless, I tend to see life visually. In this dream, I was on a beach and clouds were slowly blocking the sun as if a storm was about to come in. Then there was lightning, and rain began to fall lightly. This wasn't beautiful 30A in sunny Florida; it had more of a *Castaway* vibe minus Wilson. A really gentle voice said something like, "You're going to need to make your way to the rock over there. A storm is going to rage." The huge rock was more like a mountain jutting out of the sand. At the bottom, it had a deep cleft. I ran toward it while the rain pelted my back and hair stuck to my face, and I hid inside. It was like I was watching the troubles surrounding me and the devastation piling up. It wasn't a sign I wanted but one I would desperately need. That day I decided, *Today is the last day I'm putting my hope in my husband.*

My greatest fear was being abandoned. And the one person I loved the most was actually abandoning me. "Why are you dealing with me like this when I didn't do the bad thing?" I asked God. "I didn't cause this, as you well know." There are no emergencies to God. He doesn't drive an ambulance. He saw this coming and had made a plan for it. Above all, he would take care of me.

My formula was crumbling, but in the crumbling came the greatest gift, the thing I wear around my heart like a diamond necklace: I learned to put my hope in someone who would not abandon or fail me. This was a fork in the road of my faith, one I would constantly look back on to recall God's care. I learned over time that God was the reward—not getting my husband back. That the end was the beginning. That out of death could come life. These concepts would later permeate every aspect of my life, my parenting, my businesses, my relationships, my finances. There isn't one thing the tendrils of the gospel don't wrap themselves around and claim fiercely. And my heart was in its grip. But our marriage was not fixable. It was dead and would have to be resurrected into something new.

I painfully opened my clenched hands and said, *So be it. Your will, not mine.* I had never prayed that.

Well, I take that back. I had prayed the Lord's Prayer my whole life: "Thy will be done. Thy Kingdom come on earth as it is in heaven." My head prayed that prayer, but I had never prayed those words with my whole heart until that moment as I sat on our burnt orange couch. *You will have to show me how to do this because I don't know how to have faith like this. I can't do this anymore. This is the end.*

God showed me that I wasn't abandoned. Through the pastors who came over and helped kick my husband out because I didn't have the words. They held the door open and found him a place to stay with a seventy-year-old, widowed man whose shag carpet matched his name: Frank Brown. God took care of me through the women who came over and cleaned my house top to bottom because I could barely manage to shower.

He rebuilt my faith in his provision through the guys from our small group who came over to take the trash out. Our friend Marcus finished roofing a shed my husband had started. Friends took me out on Friday nights so I wouldn't have to be alone another weekend. God showed me compassion through my parents watching my children while I mourned and forgot to eat. "I got you a burger on my way home," my dad would say with a half smile.

In my languishing, I simply forgot to eat, to bathe, to live. But God didn't abandon me. That is why, to this day, I so meticulously seek out the lonely woman, the abandoned. I can see myself in her pretend smile and tired eyes. I know the look of someone who cries each hour as consistently as the church bells across the street ring. *You are not forgotten*, my eyes say back when I bring her the dinner she tried to tell me not to bring. "I accidentally made double."

In the first week my husband was gone, God held up the sun for me. I say that because what should have taken years, he made happen in my heart over seven days. I was staying with my parents when God began handing me different terrible things from the past, The Stupid Watch, for instance. Will you forgive him for that whopper? Sometimes I slapped God's hand away and said, "Not right now."

But as clear as day, I heard God say, "But you are your husband. And I forgive you every hour your heart wanders. Every time you prostitute yourself out for identity in reputation or money or mothering." He really used the word *prostitute* with me—the one who didn't step outside of marriage with my body, the one who stayed pure. The nerve! Except Jesus turned the tables, as he always does. I realized that God dealt with me the way I must deal with my husband: undeserved forgiveness for a sin too big to be healed.

> I realized that God dealt with me the way I must deal with my husband: undeserved forgiveness for a sin too big to be healed.

Before our marriage crumbled, I had been happily Pinteresting my brains out for the nursery decor and I had written a verse on my chalkboard that I had forgotten to erase. I have no clue why I chose it, other than the fact that God knew what was coming and provided for me before I knew I needed his provision. Again proving there are no emergencies to him.

Be kind to one another, tenderhearted, forgiving one another, as God in Christ forgave you.

Ephesians 4:32

One day during the first week from hell, I looked up and noticed that verse again. I gasped. I knew I was called to forgive, but I didn't know how. And I wasn't sure my husband deserved it. After all, he hadn't even asked for it yet. But the last part struck me: *as God in Christ forgave you.* How did God in Christ forgive me? A verse I had memorized in high school popped in my head: "While we were still sinners, Christ died for us" (Romans 5:8). *While we were still sinners.* While we actively chose our sin, God said, "I forgive you even unto my death."

In that moment, my heart was like the pumpkin-turned-carriage, mice-become-coachmen, or raggedy maid-turned-princess in *Cinderella.* It was nothing short of miraculous. I actually went looking for things to forgive. The other woman? Compassion—he must have lied to her too. She must have been deeply wounded somehow if she thought the best she could do was another woman's husband. She believed the lies. The devastating New Year's party? I forgave him for abandoning me. The watch in the family photos? I stopped in the hallway and said out loud, "You are done chasing me. I forgive him for wearing that watch." Later, I would come to find out that, on his own journey of receiving forgiveness and throwing off his sin, my husband took off the watch at a stoplight and gave it to a man on the side of the road.

There are one zillion instances of God binding up my wounds over the years, even this year where God still remembers me and shows compassion. Where he still deals with my husband's shame and covers it with love. It often happens daily over here. Some instances I hide in my heart, treasuring little mercies in the hidden corners. But most of them overwhelm me with so much gratitude that I have to share. I try to document them as best I can so everyone can benefit from the testimony of death to life. In fact, it was through this documentation on my early blog and on social media (that would surely end any Good Christian Woman reputation I had) that people were drawn to the honesty and redemption our marriage was experiencing. My influence, requests to speak, and writing opportunities grew like crazy. What I thought was my stop sign, the bitter end, was actually my catapult into writing and speaking—things that produce life and ministry for us today. Death was once again producing life. What stripped us now clothes us, and what depleted us now provides for us. The death of the mediocre marriage I thought I wanted paved the way to a thriving, more meaningful, and deeper relationship with my husband. And it doesn't stop with us. How many people have come to our living room with the same story of death and left with hope for life?

I often think about when Moses parted the Red Sea. The Israelites were at the end of themselves. There were no more steps to take except to die by the unforgiving waves in front of them or the enemy army behind them. Then God made a way by parting the sea. And because of Moses's obedience, hundreds of thousands of people made their way across to a new life. More importantly, their faith impacted generations. That is because they told the story over and over so no one would forget it. It's the same story I keep telling and will never stop: we were at our end, death was in front of us, and by a miracle we escaped.

The end was the way.

> *What I thought was my stop sign, the bitter end, was actually my catapult. Death was once again producing life.*

. . . . **Following Your Breadcrumbs** . . . .

Sometimes things in life just happen to you. You aren't planning on it, you don't want it, and you find yourself feeling shame for things you had no control over. This is difficult to dig into, but I want you to know that you're not alone. And even if you did walk right into something you knew you shouldn't have, I understand that too. We all do.

We've all had experiences that can produce embarrassment and shame. In our wisdom, we would like to bury and be done with those moments—counting them as a loss. But what if what was a loss at one point could actually be used for good?

Not everything has to be seen as that, and sometimes when it's still fresh, it can feel impossible. It reminds me of the three days when Jesus was in the tomb. What good could come out of this death? But without that death, we wouldn't have the greatest story of life ever told!

My treasure map word:
REDEMPTION

Have you ever examined places of death in your life to see how they have actually gone on to produce life? Take some time to reflect on that.

What has felt like a stop sign but could catapult you into healing and living authentically as a layered and complicated human?

Can you name your suffering—and how that suffering has led you into new empathy, new ways of trusting, either small or large?

four

The Business of Finding Yourself

Every time my sister brings a potluck item for a family dinner, she says, "I'll bring the Jesus wieners." We all know it's the famous church basement recipe: little Vienna sausages slathered in off-brand grape jelly and gently cooked on low in a Crock-Pot all morning while everyone is singing praises upstairs. She knows this church recipe by heart because 1) there are only two classy ingredients and 2) inside the church, few manuals are handed to women about anything other than child-rearing and cooking. You don't go to a wedding shower and get *10 Simple Steps to Starting Your Own Business and Alienating Yourself from the Lady Folk in Your Church*. You do get *Second Baptist's Best Basement Potluck Delicacies.**

We grew up in all kinds of charismatic churches, and there was indeed lots of freedom to express yourself in worship. That is, if you define *worship* as the forty-five minutes of song time before the sermon begins while the Crock-Pot is working its magic downstairs.

....

* Revised in 1999 to include no Jell-O molds of yore.

You could grab a ribbon and run from the front to the back if you felt like it. You could bang a tambourine offbeat. You could perform "special music" with absolutely no ability to keep a tune. How many times did my mother flick my shoulder as I was shaking from built-up laughter—silently, head in hands, trying not to look at my brother and breathing deeply? There is never a more earnest prayer than a teenager asking, "God, take the specia-music giggles from thine servant's mouth. O Lord, send thine most serious of angels to protect me."

You could also come to the front and get re-saved at every altar call just in case you had anxiety about going to hell after watching a skit set to dramatic music last week at youth group. Best option for showing how free you are is being slain in the Spirit, which simply means someone hits your head and you fall backward and hope someone catches you. It's the ultimate trust fall. If you're lucky, someone will cover your legs with a modesty scarf from a basket at the front. I'm not saying it isn't real; I'm just saying this was a normal Sunday at my church. No snakes though. #thankful

With all that freedom given during worship time no matter how young or old or your gender, the same freedom was not extended to worship through work. That concept of a worshipful life would be completely foreign to me until much later in young motherhood when I heard a woman say from the stage at a women's retreat that her work as an attorney was, in fact, worship! WHUUUT? This was mind-blowing information! The last conference I had gone to ten years before (yes, ten—after all, women don't need that much personal development!) had given me the opposite idea.

As a wedding gift, an older and very respected couple had given me and my husband two tickets to a popular traveling marriage conference. Of course, four months into marriage and 3.8 months pregnant, we had zero problems and probably could help these poor troubled couples with so many issues. At this conference, a pastor's wife pulled all the wives aside (about five hundred of us) into a breakout session and said, "The reason families are so messed up is that women leave the home to go find purpose elsewhere. They leave their children and choose to spend so much time away from them. What do you expect with no one to watch them? Women, unless there is some dire financial struggle, you need to stay in your home." Then she concluded with this damning statement: "Why even have children?"

I probably shook my head shamefully in agreement. "Why can't they just be happy at home?"

I hate to say it, but as someone privileged enough at the time to stay at home because my husband's job provided, I was perfectly happy to produce children and make sure my husband and family had a great home-cooked meal every night. That pastor's wife valued, affirmed, and scripturally bolstered my misguided opinions on where a woman belonged inside the church ecosystem. The gist of what I had constantly heard about men and women as people who followed Christ could be summed up like this: *We all have God-given roles, and if you play by these rules, you will be blessed and happy and, more importantly, no man will be harmed in your pursuit for his power. Now get out there and do good things for God—but remember, don't disrupt the system!*

"My greatest job," "my greatest calling," as many Christian books told me, was to be a mother and wife. THIS is what makes a woman useful in the ecosystem of believers. Never mind if you never get married or are unable to have children. Never mind if your marriage is ending and your life falls apart. Never mind if you have to quit your "job" as the children's ministry director because your latest pregnancy has you vomiting thirty-two times during a church meeting. Never mind if you went to college and your parents spent thousands upon thousands for you to teach high school English. Never mind if God gave you gifts and talents beyond mothering and being a wife.

For a while I was mostly joyful and compliant in mothering and wife-ing. Except I found a loophole that was acceptable in the Christian community: a side hustle! Yes, perfectly acceptable to have a cutesy painting business where I would paint children's names using heinous stencils to hang in nurseries. It was my own hobby, it didn't bother anyone, and gosh darn it, people thought I was good at it.

One day—I don't know what got into me (was it what the men called "ambition"?)—I went to a local boutique in a fancier shopping area and asked the owner if I could paint signs for her clients. I had pictures of my works in an album and examples she could hang at the store. She would take half, and I would make approximately $5.75 on each sign after buying materials. Totally worth the three hours it took me to make each sign! Regardless, it was something to do that was my own. And I relished it.

After realizing that particular business was not worth my time, I asked for a camera for Christmas. It was a big ask: three hundred dollars! I started taking photos of my children and then posting them to my blog. I was a .blogspot, not a .com, for way too long (it cost money to be a .com). I would write stories about the photos, some funny, some serious. And something interesting started happening: people asked me to take their photos. I did them for free at first and then decided—ever so begrudgingly, thinking it might be wrong—to charge people a small amount for my time. These chunks of cash were exhilarating to me. It was like selling rocks but with a real product people needed, and it was giving me life. *I can't believe people pay me to do this!*

I became more and more successful at it. A woman I didn't know contacted me and said, "I wasn't going to have any photos taken for my second wedding, but my niece has convinced me something would be better than nothing!" Was this a backhanded compliment? Sure! But I wasn't a professional wedding photographer, and I wasn't offended. She would take a risk on me, and I would risk ruining her wedding day with my mediocre skills. My camera sucked with the night shots and that's when I used that wedding money to buy a better camera body and more lenses. Suddenly, I was busy every weekend at shoots. Family shoots became wedding shoots, and I took on my sister as a business partner. It was fun to scale something of my own. I knew I shouldn't be having this much fun, but if I just kept quiet about it and it wasn't my full-time job, I wouldn't disrupt the Christian Culture Ecosystem. Except little by little my heart was growing more confident and less dependent on what people inside the church thought I should be.

Meanwhile, as I mentioned before, I was posting these shoots and honest commentary below them. This apparently made my blog sort of funny and entertaining, and I seemed to be helping people feel not so alone in motherhood, in wife-ing, in the ecosystem. One of our male friends said to me, "Lindsay was showing me your blog. I can't believe you have four hundred followers! Do you know any of them?"

> *Little by little my heart was growing more confident and less dependent on what people inside the church thought I should be.*

"No! Isn't that crazy? Someone other than my mom is reading. Go figure," I said, basking in my new life as a local celebrity.

All sarcasm aside, people *were* noticing me. Which I did feel sort of proud about, but it got quickly covered in a little evangelical-lady shame. I was taking time away from my children to go on these shoots, and I was spending time making graphics and a website when my husband got home from work. I was also spending money on my "hobbies" that made money. Even worse, I enjoyed time away from my children and husband! I decided it wasn't so wrong because I wasn't "full-time," and I was a better mother and wife when I engaged in my gifts.

I was living my full and happy life. But it started to feel too full. While I could have scaled the photography business, I had started yet another accidental side business: I now had to keep up with my social media presence, and I was pregnant with our third. I couldn't handle it all, so I handed the business over to my sister, who was better at it than I was anyway. I felt a little sad about this, but I thought, somewhere in the back of my head, *This isn't your calling; it's a bridge.* This self-awareness was a godsend as I continued to maneuver business changes; nothing was ever wasted and nothing was ever lost on God, even in the moment when it felt like I was letting go of something great. This little stop sign would make more room for me to catapult into something even better.

I had babies, we renovated houses, and I was the room mom at school. I continued making meal plans while my husband was working hard in the corporate world. Still, I couldn't quit my cute little side hustles. I would let go of one, then pick another up. I couldn't quit entrepreneuring online but didn't quite know why. Even when, from the pulpit, our pastor slammed social media as a waste of time and particularly a trap for *our* women. "We have these so-called Christian women who are leading other Christian women astray! Because women are so lost in social media, they're listening to false prophets. These women with so much influence on Instagram—with their long captions." I felt like melting into my seat. *Me, the queen of long captions. And that platform, which I consider one of my greatest ministries. A complete waste of time?* He went on to directly mention names of prominent women in the faith sphere on social media who were poisoning other women. I swear at one point he made direct eye contact with me. When the last *worship* song was playing, I excused myself and quickly walked into the bathroom, where I cried so hard that I knew I would have to leave early and sit in the car while my husband picked up the kids from Sunday school. *How unmotherly of me!*

The year before, I had gone to a business conference of one of the women the pastor had mentioned to learn how to better lean into my gifts and use them in business. Nothing existed like this inside the church, so I had thought it would do for now. Said woman didn't mention her faith all that much, but I wasn't there to learn about God necessarily. I was there to learn how to strategically grow my social media influence and business.

Sobbing in the church bathroom, I knew I had been outed as one of those deceptively influential women right then and there. A friend of a friend followed me into the bathroom—I think to confront me on being too much *out there* and possibly falling into this "false prophet's" grip. Yet, when I looked at her in the mirror with red puffy eyes and smeared mascara, she relented. I already felt so small and so publicly marked with the scarlet letter *E* for too Extra, too Entrepreneurial, and too Entitled to be free of the Ecosystem.

Why in the world did I feel so free to be me outside of the church and not inside it? It was becoming a point of contention, and I started to speak up about it with friends. "Is this a thing for you too?" Of course it was. We were all trying to be faithful in our church community, but to fit inside those doors, we had to shrink so small.

Yet like a runaway train, I couldn't stop myself or my businesses from growing. At this point, my next cute side hustle was joining a full-blown, multimillion-dollar network marketing business. Enter pyramid scheme/snake oil jokes also hurled from the pulpit in an attempt to shame women for thriving in a business where they could stay at home *and* make money. (Hey look, my dream of being a snake handler in church finally came true!)

After I had just had my fourth baby, I started thinking of getting some help with the kids. I was managing ten thousand customers and empowering hundreds of leaders growing along with me, working forty-plus hours a week while nursing and running kids around. I had never even toyed with the idea of hiring help. The ticker tape at the bottom of my brain had been glowing with judgment for years. "Why even have kids?!" But my husband, in sales himself, encouraged me. "You are not a bad mom for getting help. Your business is growing faster than mine. I can't imagine trying to grow like that while doing all you do. Let's get you a nanny!"

Getting a nanny after my fourth baby so I could dedicate time to growing a new business—like any man in the world might do—was like announcing a third nipple. You just don't. Cover that thing up and alter every single shirt you wear to hide the deformity. Trouble was, "my deformity" was now surpassing even my husband's paycheck by double and allowing me to thrive and grow.*

I had rarely been part of any kind of organization that didn't squelch women; this business was built on women *and* was constantly building them up. I am assuming men have understood this kind of investment in their professional and personal lives for a while now, but this was news to me. It was like I was living in a dream world where I could be me—in fact, the company needed me to be me! They sent me on trips for achieving big goals, places I never thought we could go. Traveling was a little lost love of mine I had never voiced.

> *As God does, he flips the script and gives us new eyewear, maybe new eyeballs.*

Finally, I understood the glimmer in my friend's eye when she was on photoshoots doing what she was made to do. I had the glimmer now, and nothing could take it out of my eye. I was feeling so free.

It didn't happen in the environment I thought it would. I thought I would find it inside my church walls with the red carpet and the dark wooden pews and the people all in their designated places wearing half smiles, *worshiping*. But as God does, he flips the script and gives us new eyewear, maybe new eyeballs. Maybe a pair of wings. And sends us flying so we're singing our songs above the trees, up into the sky. Maybe, when God closes a heavy, wooden church door, he opens a stained-glass window to fly through.

---

* A year or so later, it also allowed me to retire my husband from corporate America.

Following Your Breadcrumbs

When I was young, our house had a laundry chute that was probably eight feet long. At the bottom of the chute was a giant, industrial rolling basket always filled to the brim with the dirty clothes of ten people. Because we were "spirited children" with "incredible creativity" and also "terrible siblings," we would dangle our toddler sister down the chute while she cackled and fell into the soft pile of disgusting garments. As she got older, she no longer fit in the chute—and my mother hollered at us when my sister sort of got stuck once. Good news though: she eventually wiggled her way out of what could have been a call to the fire department!

Something I had a hard time reconciling as I matured as a woman of God was that I no longer fit in a church that thrust me into the pews for so long. I was valued and cherished outside the church doors, and people were willing to invest in me. Inside the church was a stark contrast: few resources were offered because I wasn't important enough to be resourced. But that sent me on a journey to ask God what he truly says and thinks about women. I read the biblical stories about how Christ treated the marginalized, which were often women. Then there's the parable of the wedding feast. The list is full of the castoffs: "Go out quickly to the streets and lanes of the city, and bring in the poor and crippled and blind and lame" (Luke 14:21). That's good news for those of us who tend to feel shame for not quite fitting the "Christian" woman expectation list all the time. Even when others have made us not feel welcomed, we're on the invitation list! It's almost unbelievable.

It's important to believe you're a part of a great royal family and you serve a loving, good, generous King who is watching you. I don't mean watching as in waiting for you to fail so he can provide swift judgment. No, he's watching you, and he can't stop smiling. You are cared for, noticed, loved. You have a place. And you have a purpose. Discovering what that is can be as simple as the answers you give to these next two questions.

My treasure map word:
HARD WORKER

When you look back on your life, when did you feel the most free?

What if those moments were meant to be a big arrow indicating DO MORE OF THIS?

five

A Tale of Two Bosses

noticed the blinking light on my phone. I must have missed a call on the drive to my brand-new student teaching assignment. *Who in the world called me from Emporia? I swear, if it's Dan telling me how I ruined his life with our breakup again, I might throw this thing in a random kid's locker on the way to room 191.* I listened to the message before I stepped through the door amid the slamming metal lockers and overuse of cologne. "We need you to come into the Admissions Advisory Office as soon as you can make it in." What was this all about? *You can't fail student teaching before you even start, can you? Is it these flats I stole from my mom? They do deserve an F-.* I hung up my tiny flip phone. I was too nervous to think about it. Today and for the next couple of months, I would be learning how to manage a classroom full of hormonally expressive high school juniors and seniors.

Together, we would explore the wonder of literature and grammar using a magical cheating tool called SparkNotes.* You don't even have to read a book anymore. You can just go to a website that

---

* Don't tell your high schooler . . . although they probably already know.

sums up what happened in each chapter and provides the underlying themes. It's made by cheaters for cheaters (and I happened to use it a lot to get through college). Truth be told, I mostly loved writing, but I didn't have the attention span or interest for the incessant reading of the classics like my peers did. I didn't know why people constantly had their heads in memoirs and historical fiction. Why not spend your time traveling to Spain, or working and making money to take a road trip to San Diego, or decoupaging your apartment walls with vintage fashion patterns and broken mirror pieces (including the ceiling fan, I'm sure my landlord was pleased)?* For student teaching, I would basically be reading the assignments with the students. The slight caveat? I was also teaching it. If you're wondering if that was my real plan, um, yep, that was my actual real and working plan to get through the semester.

The first couple of weeks in the classroom were a snooze fest. I sat in the back while Ms. Anita Porter—with short curly white hair and tan flax dresses with flowy pants underneath—taught yawn-worthy lessons on plurals (plurals's? plurals'? plurai?). She didn't give me any tasks nor any instruction. Did she even know I was there? Finally, she let me grade vocab tests and retrieve coffee for her from the mysterious and always unwelcoming teachers' lounge. Bored out of my mind with truly nothing else to do, I noticed the seating arrangement on the pile of papers strewn about the desk. *The key to controlling the classroom!* So I spent thirty-five minutes each class memorizing the names and placements. They were learning parts of speech, and I was learning this particular classroom's biome—the faces and mannerisms. I am the first to admit that I am terrible at names and memorization, but an angel of the Lord must have equipped me for that moment: *This is your way in.* On a Friday, I worked up enough courage to walk to the door right before dismissal. The usually stone-faced teens weren't quite sure

----

* What a landlord's dream I was!

60

of what to do with this silent owl who usually perched at the desk in the back.

"Goodbye, Michelle. Later, Andy! And you're Michael, but it appears everyone calls you Mikey. Chevon. Marissa . . ." and on and on twenty-seven times. Their eyes grew big as they left the classroom.

On the twenty-eighth time, a ragtag smaller guy dressed with a skater vibe, pocket chain, and long, stringy hair unfolded his crossed arms and barely, just barely, made eye contact with me. "Ms. Baker, right? That was actually pretty rad."

And the stoic Ms. Porter with her demure pen clicking, turned her lip up slightly, "Well done in establishing the kind of classroom you want to have. Tomorrow you will start teaching the first part of our class. You can do the grammar icebreaker."

Beaming, I sat there. *I can do this. Except I'm really terrible at grammar. And don't people have editors for this? Can I hire an editor for my classroom? At least I'll get to do something, anything, besides staring at the clock. And anyway, I'm sure she'll help me figure it out.*

Apparently, that smallest bout of obviously divine intervention made my supposed mentor teacher really confident in my skills. But I crushed the daily grammar quizzes I had found online (with answer keys). The next week, she told me I would be teaching *The Adventures of Huckleberry Finn*. And because I hadn't read that book since, oh, ten years earlier, I took to SparkNotes for the condensed cheater's version of chapter 1. I wondered if Ms. Porter would catch on. Ironically, little did I know, Ms. Porter was about to pull an old Tom Sawyer on me: she abruptly stopped showing up to the classroom AT ALL. As in, she was reading novels in the teachers' lounge and rarely checked in with me except to pop her head in sideways with a sigh and say, "I do worry about the noise level in here some days."

I had no clue what I was doing, but being a mere four years older than some of these kids, I knew what they needed to know before they entered college (90 percent of them were going). I had an inkling at this point that I didn't really want to teach high school English or be in a formal classroom setting, but I did like teaching something. So I taught to their next phase of life, not to the tests they'd be taking at the end of the year. (Anita could take the hit for that.) I simply wanted them to know how to write a good paper (the unsung art of a thesis), how to expand their vocabulary (a lifelong skill), and how to understand an author's perspective (remain curious). They would be successful if they could do those three things, so I made a deal with myself and with them, even if they didn't know it: fake it out of that classroom alive, and we all win.

There were days when the kids left the classroom and I stood at the podium and cried out of sheer overwhelm before the next class arrived. There were days I laughed a lot and found joy in the quirkiness of the awkward-teenager stage. There were days I felt fulfilled. I had never felt more exhausted in my life, creating all this new material and doing it pretty much alone. My "mentor" teacher was nowhere to be found.

I was so busy that I forgot all about the college adviser's office call. Until one day I finally did answer, "Hello, yes! SO sorry, I have been meaning to call you all back. I'm assuming I didn't fill out my graduation form properly?"

"Well, actually, *we've* made a mistake," Barbara said. "Somehow, we missed requiring a class last semester to make sure you can graduate. We have a teacher willing to let you take their class remotely. You'll have to read the materials and turn in the essays throughout this semester, and you'll have to come here to take the final." I stared at the wall. This is the part of the dream where you wake up. *Surely this is one of my many recurring stress nightmares where I lose all my teeth or I accidentally skip a class and can't get my diploma.*

"The class is Young Adult Literature."

I busted out a laugh. "You've got to be kidding me. I'm taking a class on how to teach the class I'm already teaching?!"

"It is *rather* ironic. But unfortunately, it must be done. Can you handle this? I'll enroll you today. You'll have some catching up to do, but we can make it happen."

Can I handle this? I'm teaching a class I somehow missed in college, and I'm doing it practically alone because Anita is seventy and retiring and busting out her final days reading novels amid the hum of the teachers' lounge fridge. Sure, Barbara, it's fine!

"Yes, I think I can make it happen!" I squeaked out. Except I couldn't make it happen.

That semester, I did not turn in a single assignment for my remote class. I couldn't. I was knee-deep in *The Great Gatsby*, in teaching four classes, in learning everything for the first time as a teacher, in figuring out if I wanted to be a teacher, in questioning whether I *should* even be allowed to be a teacher.

In the theme of faking it out alive, I bought a cheap ring from Walmart and made up a story about my fiancé, who was a doctor, errrr, a dentist (both doctors, amiright) in hopes of keeping yet another senior from asking me to prom. I bought sweater vests (sweater vests!) to look older so teachers would stop stopping me in the hallway, asking, "Where's your hall pass, young lady?" At one point, my car broke down and my mom had to drop me off at school and pick me up. Like the rest of the high schoolers. "You're literally the biggest con artist of all time," I told myself as she pulled up. "You're a literal child. You don't know what you're doing."

But I kept waking up and kept showing up. Even though I apparently didn't have college credit hours to teach young adult literature, I felt like I was finding my stride. In reading the books alongside them, I was discovering my own aha moments. For vocabulary, I made them get into groups to create art pieces that described their words. Then we hung them up all over the classroom so they could use them as references for the quiz.

We made posters and projects and I played parts of movies to educate them on stereotypes.* Suddenly, the kids were quoting my favorite movies in the class. "As IF, Ms. Baker." I was having fun. I

---

* If you're wondering, *Mean Girls* and *Clueless* really drill down this concept.

wasn't going to graduate with the credits I needed, but I was learning a lot, and they were too. I also realized that I didn't want that degree anyway. It was sort of a good feeling to at least determine what I *wasn't* going to do—high school English—even though I really, REALLY wanted to know what I would eventually do. But then, like Huck or Gatsby, it wouldn't be a coming-of-age journey if I had all the answers.

I became okay with the idea that what felt like a directional mistake could possibly be used for my and even others' good. That I was in process and, while very uncomfortable, it was truly necessary and good—even if no one was helping me figure it out. No, this wasn't what I was going to do with the rest of my life, but maybe it wasn't a mistake. When I acknowledged this, I began to feel like less of a fraud.

As the semester was coming to a close, my student teaching adviser came to watch me teach a class for my final. I had a video ready; it wouldn't play. I did an impression of the scene using my hands aggressively. It's hard to ignore a teacher with aggressive hand motions.

> *I became okay with the idea that what felt like a directional mistake could possibly be used for my and even others' good.*

The copy machine also didn't work that morning, so any unlucky student who accidentally made eye contact with me would have to read the article I had for us. Things weren't going the way I planned at all, and I was disappointed.

The kids sensed we were being watched and that it was important. One by one, the quietest boys in the back raised their hands. "Ms. Baker, do you think Gatsby knew he was doomed?" "What does the word *supercilious* mean in that last chapter?" I had never had more participation in the classroom. They were pulling for me. Mikey raised his hand and asked if I would be going to prom that weekend. "Yes, I will be there giving Breathalyzers to my sweet students. Can't wait!"

At the end of the class, my adviser sat in the back corner. He was smiling big. "Well, Ms. Baker. This is what being a teacher is. You plan things, and they go wrong—all the time. A lot of the time. But you still taught the lesson for the day. These kids are engaged! You're doing it. You're going to do well for yourself." He patted me on the back and walked out.

I don't remember much of this college adviser/professor. In fact, I can't remember his name. But I do remember he sat on his desk in the only class I ever loved in college (besides sociology): creative writing. Sitting on his desk one morning, he stopped to say, "Everyone has something to say. That will come as you keep writing. But you'll get lost if you try to write what you think others want to read. Just write what you know."* And the story being written right then and there in Ms. Porter's classroom was that I wasn't going to be a high school English teacher, but I was going to teach something. I actually liked teaching, but maybe the subject matter and audience were off.

Anita had been pretending to grade papers while she eavesdropped on the convo with my adviser. She lifted an eye from the opposite corner of the classroom, her pen never stopping. I thought she might, just maybe, finally pay me a compliment. Or, I don't know, say, *Thank you for running this class all by yourself, while I started my retirement early and ate snacks at my leisure and you could hardly find time to use the restroom.*

"Listen, I know you have to graduate in three weeks, but I was thinking I might just pay you to stay here and finish the year. I'm retiring this year anyway, and I just don't think I have it in me to finish this thing out." I laughed and inner-eye-rolled. I gave forty-three excuses for why I wouldn't be able to do that: I was in a breakup, I had no car, *our pets' heads are falling off.*** Not to mention it's illegal-ish?

....

* I think about this a lot, even now, twenty years later.
** See *Dumb and Dumber*

On my last day of student teaching, as I was packing up my things over the course of the day, I thought about the semester. How I didn't even have the credit hours to graduate as a teacher. How this job wasn't for me because I'm not smart enough or well-read enough. How I just couldn't wait to get out of there. *What a waste, I'm not even going to be a teacher. My parents are going to kill me!*

The kids brought me treats and had a little going-away party, and I reassured them that now that they knew how to write a good paper with well-formed ideas *and* had memorized key lines from *Mean Girls*, they really would be just fine in college. After the final bell rang, a student came up to me and said, "Hey, you're like, the smartest person I know . . ."

I audibly giggled at her opinion of me. *Ahhh, if you only knew.*

". . . and I think maybe I could teach one day since now I know it could be fun. I used to think books were stupid but, like, I think I like the stories and the details or whatever. Anyway, there's a party tonight at my house and you should come." She giggled through her nose. "I'm sure you don't always wear these nerdy clothes."

I could feel my eyes watering even with the backhanded compliment. "You're very sweet. I will let you borrow this sweater vest anytime—as you know, I have it in multiple colors. And hey, I know whatever you do, you're going to be really good at it. *Just keep writing what you know.*"

Maybe I'm not a fake? My "mistake" helped one girl figure something out for herself. Maybe someone would eventually come along and help me.

Over that summer, I planned to finish the actual Young Adult Literature class to complete the three hours I needed to get a diploma while I figured out what in the world I wanted to do. I had no real plan, except to not go back into the classroom. I had been nannying off and on for a family all through high school and college, and as I sat perplexed in their living room, explaining my dilemma, Mrs. Horner's lip turned up, and there was a little twinkle in her eye. "Our church is looking for a new children's ministry director, and

I think you would actually be just perfect. I mean, they won't pay much, but it will get you through."

My heart leapt. *Oh my gosh. I've been saved!* Relief washed over me. I might have a job. I could deal with little kids and teaching them about Noah's ark. Surprisingly, I got the job. Then I had the lingering thought: *Wait, am I a scam artist? Should I read about how to be in ministry or something? Here I am faking it again. Lord, how do I get myself in all these situations I'm not prepared for?*

But this time I wasn't on my own. My new boss saw my potential. Only a few months into my new job as children's ministry director (have I mentioned that I had no theological training?), my pastor, Jay Fowler, let me know it would be my turn to preach the sermon in "big church" on the importance of children and their faith. *Um, no, no, no. You don't want me up there. What are parents going to learn from me? First of all, I am not a public speaker, and second, I just want to do funny puppet shows for the kids.* "I know you can do this," he said as he walked out of my office to his next meeting with his genuine smile.

AGH!*

So I went out and did what anyone would do to prepare for their first big speaking gig—I bought an Isaac Mizrahi seersucker pantsuit from Target because I could at least look like I knew what I was doing even though I most certainly did *not*.

With a few good jokes, I stumbled through most of it, but I *did it*. Not because I was good at it and not because I was theologically sound at twenty-two years of age. I certainly didn't do it because I was ready. I did it because someone called me up and because someone removed themselves from the spotlight and gave me the chance. Someone believed something about me before I believed it myself: that I could get up there and say something important. That I had something to teach. The audacity of those first years in my career tucked something away in my heart: capable, treasured, needed,

---

* Rule 1 as church worker: only sort of cuss, but don't go all the way.

included. This boss gave me space and encouragement to figure it out. I may have felt like I was faking it, but maybe that's what everyone felt like when they were learning something new. Cue The Dixie Chicks for dramatic effect: "*Wide open spaaaaaaces, room to make her big mistakes.*"

Over the next couple of years, my boss sent me to various trainings and conferences and paid for it (*what?!*). I also needed to read *this* book and *that* one about the importance of children's ministry. In fact, I was going to have to lead the discussion at the next team meeting. I made my own curriculum. I took kids to get ice cream. I ran an after-school program. I made my parents do a puppet show with me in which they threw candy at the kids and it hit a child in the eye. Battle wounds for the Lord! I was also falling in love with my soon-to-be husband and sort of with the adult person I was in the process of becoming. I didn't have to be comfortable in every environment that wasn't familiar. In fact, not having all the answers and not knowing everything became sort of untroubling.

But mostly, I think I fell in love with leadership, which is a form of teaching, after watching my boss lead through serving others. I had never had a boss who cared so much for my heart while asking me to do things I didn't know I was capable of doing. He told me repeatedly that my job was the most important one at the church (I couldn't believe he was sharing so much "power" with me). He said all that with a toothpick in his mouth (which might as well have been a cigarette in an old Western) while sipping his fifth Diet Coke of the day, a tenderness in his voice that came from his heart or the aspartame. And I loved him because he knew the whole time, without me saying anything, that I thought I was faking it. He knew it because he had been on my side of the table a few times. He knew I wondered if I had it in me. I wondered if I was worthy of all this empowering importance and genuine care and concern. Unlike being left alone in a classroom with no guidance, he showed me the way. Like the old movie ushers with flashlights in a dark theater leading me to a great movie that was just beginning.

I am still three hours short of my teaching degree because Young Adult Literature is incomplete on my college record. But those two bosses were part of the greatest course on how to be a young adult. I learned that faking it to become the person I was supposed to be is not really fraud, and I found (or was it they who found me?) trustworthy Sherpas along the way, gently prodding me up the mountain I was so unsure of.

Following Your Breadcrumbs

I went to a party once where I only knew one person, the person who invited me. I was in Chicago for a conference and was bored anyway, so I hopped in my rental car and drove to the suburbs. When I arrived, the host was filling plastic cups with wine and happily serving pizza. I recognized her. She had just made The New York Times *bestseller list for a book about undercomplicating hosting (coincidentally). There was karaoke, nothing too out of the ordinary, except the people on the mic were well-known recording artists. In the other corner was a CEO of a major tech company talking with people who were throwing their heads back cackling. I stood there thinking I was in a dream.*

There have been many times in life when I looked around and asked, "How in the world did I even get here? I don't belong with these people. Everyone here knows or does all the things better than I do. I bet no one here is wearing their underwear backward like I am." Turns out that we all have those same thoughts (minus the underwear?). Being in these situations is a breeding ground for learning and growth. And sometimes, you find someone who will come alongside you to tell you that you are meant to be there.

My treasure map word:
TEACHER

For me, in each of the teaching instances—a not helpful "boss" and a truly invested boss—I felt like I was faking it! But I learned something about myself and even gained a couple of helpful skills. Good or bad, they both shaped me. However, the good boss called me up and saw something in me I didn't quite see yet and pointed me in the right direction of my true calling. Who has nudged or pushed you in the right direction? Looking back, who have those people been, and what have they seen in you?

When was a time you felt like an impostor? What were you "faking" that was really just the beginning of something new? (I'm not talking about the real faking it where you put on a front just to impress others!)

What was the potential that you couldn't see then but that pointed to something true in who you were to become?

PART 2

Where You Are

six

A Basket, a Frozen Pizza, a Front Yard

Do not neglect to show hospitality to strangers, for thereby some have entertained angels unawares.

Hebrews 13:2

Growing up, I knew what having out-of-town guests meant—I had the biggest room, with a bathroom attached. *With the biggest room comes the greatest responsibilities to your extended Texan family and friends . . . Proverbs 500.* I would become a drifter in my own home for three to five days, going door to door pitifully asking to sleep on someone's squeaky trundle bed.

My room had to be spotless: clean sheets, thirty-seven pillows on the bed, and a medium-to-large-sized snack basket awaiting the guests. Imagine what it was like when I first traveled somewhere else. No mints on the bed?! No giant snack basket?! No spiced cinnamon donuts from the local pumpkin patch that provided my entire daily caloric needs? Without eating every three hours, how will I have the energy to lie poolside for the next three days?* The service in suburban Wisconsin is appalling, honestly.

We didn't just host travelers; we also invited in the Mormons or the Jehovah's Witnesses, my dad's blind friend from law school (more on that later) or the disheveled neighbor kid, and there was always a stray cat under the table that my mother was nursing back to health.

"We have learned Marty has leukemia. I didn't know cats could get leukemia, but I spent about $565 finding out," she said, exasperated while wiping her hands on her apron.

"Oh, that's terrible! Gosh, Mom. How did you even know?"

"Well, I made your father go in the drainage pipe under the driveway because she hadn't come out for two days."

On most days, I was gone at school and then soccer practice, so I usually rolled in right around dinner. I never knew who I would find at the table. Just our family of ten, a neighbor, a missionary with different beliefs, a relative stopping through, a cat with leukemia? All I knew was that dinner at home was a requirement. No excuses!

I'd walk into the house all sweaty, throw down my bags, and enter the kitchen ready to eat fifty-six pounds of spaghetti. My mom always made large dinners for guests: homemade rolls, brisket, twice-baked potatoes, and chocolate chip cookies.** Then breakfast: cinnamon rolls and an egg casserole. You would have thought she owned a bed and breakfast. People came in and out of our home, sharing meals, playing dominoes, and telling stories well into the night around the long, wooden farmhouse table my mother had bought at a garage sale. And this was before it was cool to write *gather* on everything. She was actually *gathering*! I didn't always know who the guests were, but they all seemed happy to be there: the traveling preacher, the Mormon missionaries, or the person selling us a vacuum—all pretty much the same to me.

* How is anyone supposed to sleep with just one pillow and one blanket?!
** Now I'm drooling. Is it dinnertime?

76

". . . and Elder Johnson, if you only believe in one God, why do you believe you'll become a mini-god when you go to heaven? Wouldn't you have to believe in other gods besides the one true God? This doesn't sound monotheistic to me, as you have previously claimed," Linus, also known as my dad, would ask.

The eighteen-year-old boys with matching military-style haircuts, pressed white shirts, and black-and-white name tags would stop midchew, unsure how to respond. "Jami, you're in eighth grade. What do you think: polytheistic or monotheistic?" I could see their wheels turning like my own as I snapped out of wondering why the name tags began with *Elder* when they were clearly missing their mothers, the way they scarfed down a home-cooked meal. *I guess we're all in Linus's seminary now.*

"Well, Dad, when you put it that way, it does sound like more than one God," I said smugly, adding a brand-new set of words to my vocabulary that no other thirteen-year-old would ever use in daily conversation.

This was just normal. Although I'm sure it wasn't normal how the missionaries got banned from our house after their tenth visit because their leaders realized their conversion project was backfiring, and now their missionaries were asking questions about their faith.* Regardless, our home had a revolving door. And with ten people in our family, my mother was constantly trying to keep the house from looking like a bull had a gin and tonic in the china cabinet while a tornado had ripped through the dining room. Often, it just was a mess, no matter how hard she tried to get us to put away our things. But it didn't stop her and my dad from continually inviting people in.

When my husband and I began our own family in a 1,000-square-foot ranch, we started to host regularly. His Filipino background is all about gathering constantly with family and friends, so together, we didn't know any other way but to open our doors. Don't be fooled.

....

* Yes, that happened. Our family was "fired" from being on the Mormon missionary list. Unconvertible apparently.

We had a budget of -$100, so birthday parties were strategically scheduled after lunchtime and always ended before dinner to save on food costs. If we wanted to have dinner with friends, we definitely couldn't afford to go out, so we'd invite everyone over for a potluck. I was always pregnant or breastfeeding, and so were my friends, so we weren't spending money on alcohol. Dessert was always my famous chocolate chip cookies because they were cheap to make.*

At a giant first birthday party for our first child, I remember complaining to my mother that our house was so small, and we had the budget to match. "Look around," she said. "Everyone is having a great time. The best parties are when everyone is jam-packed in a room with nowhere to go but right there with each other. Those are some of my favorite memories when your dad and I had all you little kids." I tucked that away. I knew she was saying that people don't care about your house. They just want to be with you. So in each life stage and in each financial season, no matter the size of the house, the doors remained open. Fifteen years later, I know what my mother said is true.

Sometimes when something comes easily for you, you end up being the one who does that thing the most out of your friends and family. It can be lopsided. Early on I sometimes wondered why people didn't invite us over even though we had had them over twenty times. It never occurred to me that it might not be natural for them. So it was a surprise to discover, when we moved into our current house on Bradford Place, that our seasoned neighbors had a rotating dinner party for the better part of twenty years. They threw us into the mix before we had even officially moved in. They brought out their fine china, which made me extremely self-conscious (was I supposed to register for that when we got married? Oops!). They split up the couples to different tables, so we had to get to know each

---

* Technically, they are my mom's famous chocolate chip cookies. I stole the recipe and memorized it, as it was all I ate in college (my freshman fifteen proved it).

—— THE Best Chocolate Chip Cookies ——

Throw all of this in your mixer IMMEDIATELY and send flowers later to my current address:

> 2 sticks butter, softened
> 1 cup brown sugar
> 1 cup sugar

Mix the first three ingredients well. Then to that mix, add:

> 1 tsp vanilla
> 1 tsp salt
> 1 tsp baking soda

Mix again. Then add:

> 2 eggs

Mix on low until egg is just mixed in. Don't over mix, or you're not going to heaven. (Fine, that's not true but you will have tough cookies.) To that mix add:

> 2½ to 3 cups flour

Start with 2½ cups and see if the dough is really sticky. If it is, add the remaining ½ cup. Then add:

> ½ bag chocolate chips

Do not overmix! Yes, I am bossy. I make my cookies oversized. They are better this way. Trust me and the extra ten pounds I have hanging around.

The secret is to make the cookies ginormous and bake at 350°F for 11 minutes until there is BARELY a tiny bit of brown on some of the tops. You almost want them to look a little undercooked because they cook a tad more on the pan when you take them out. Let them sit for a couple minutes before digging in.

Ahhh, soft, chewy love.

Then have someone else clean up. You are welcome.

other without the crutch of our spouse close by. This was their way, and I was just a guest.

We spent the night laughing and hearing all about the people we would live closest to for hopefully the next decade, and they made sure to tell us about the infamous white elephant party. "The biggest prize you can win that night is the stuffed squirrel. No one knows why, but we all fight for it pretty hard. Loretta usually ends up with it, though, because no one wants to compete with her fierce love for the thing."

I looked over and saw my husband's competitive heart flutter. "Loretta, you'd let me have a year with the squirrel, wouldn't you?" he said with a wink.

"Notta chance, Mark!"

Only six months out from the next Christmas party, and my husband was talking trash to our seventy-year-old neighbor. While no one there was our age, I loved seeing photos of their grandchildren and hearing about their retirement plans and trips. It didn't matter that their homes weren't updated with the latest trends or that their kids were grown. Likely, if we weren't neighbors, we wouldn't have found enough common ground to be friends. As people moved and the demographic of the neighborhood got younger, I couldn't help but be thankful for these quarterly dinner parties that forced us to get to know each other.

When the house across the street went up for sale, I noticed a young family driving by regularly and going to showings.* I "happened" to waddle my four-hundred-month pregnant belly out to the mailbox when they drove up.

"Hi. I'm Jami! Will you hurry up and buy this house already?!" I yelled.

The woman busted out laughing. "Well, I like you already. Cute baby bump! I'm Kristen. It's just that I'm not sure about the backyard. It slopes and backs to the creek. Makes me nervous for my twins."

....

* Like the nosy neighbor I am, I always look out the blinds when a car drives up the street.

"Lucky for you, we play mostly in our front yard. And there's this awesome dinner club that we do quarterly, just this street. And we're here! I have four wild children . . . we will entertain your twins. Just trust me. You gotta be on this street!"

The next month, they moved in. I couldn't have been more thrilled and also slightly irritated that I didn't make a commission off that home sale. *I totally closed the deal.* But who needs a commission when you finally have a new neighbor who is your age with little kids? I had my fourth baby that summer. I remember breastfeeding while walking past a window looking for my six-year-old, Lila. Out of the corner of my eye, I saw her across the street. *She must have escaped when I fell asleep!*

I opened the door and saw Kristen having a lengthy conversation with her despite the blaring cicadas. Lila was shirtless, wearing mismatched princess plastic heels, a karate bandana, and a tutu skirt.

Mortified, shirt lifted, baby suckling, my misshapen tummy hanging out, and my two-day-old mascara smeared, I yelled out the side door, "Kristen! I'm so sorry. Can you send Lila back home? Lila, what on the good Lord's earth are you wearing?!"

Kristen laughed, unbothered. "Girl, I get it. I'm bringing her over. Can I hold the baby while you sleep or shower or hide in your room?" It was the start of something so rich.

More and more, the neighborhood hospitality grew. It was interesting how doing the thing that was natural for me sparked others to join in their own ways. We began hanging out even when there wasn't a dinner party. We started a "Freezer Friday" where we would pull things out of the fridge or freezer. The rule: you had to use what you had on hand—no one could spend time making anything. We set chairs and tables at the bottom of the driveway while the kids scootered by or fought with one another and learned about "street justice." The most unlikely of groups was

> *It was interesting how doing the thing that was natural for me sparked others to join in their own ways.*

81

forming despite us being a mixed bag of Democrats, Republicans, hippies, mainstreamers, and even Worcestershire lovers. We texted each other throughout the week: "MAYDAY! I need two eggs" or "Anyone want these books my kids have grown out of?"

Just like 9/11, we all remember where we were and what we were doing when we got the shelter-in-place order at the start of the COVID-19 pandemic. While watching the news, I thought: *How will we do this alone? I need my people. I need them near.* Thanks to the text strand, we kept up with one another. If someone was going to the store, they asked the others what they needed. One neighbor let us pick fabric for masks and sewed them up quickly. Everyone was swapping items from their pantries* and sharing the most precious resource: toilet paper! The generous spirit remained even when it came to our behinds.

As time dragged on, one of the neighbors lost her dear mother-in-law, and we all ached for her. She was now in charge of the tedious and sad task of going through her mother-in-law's belongings. I remember staring off into the distance and thinking, *What can we do? There has to be something.* Like in a cheesy Hallmark movie, my pile of baskets across the room came into focus. To know me is to know that I love all things old, and what's better than old things but collecting lots of them? I love baskets; they're good for everything: laundry, toys, rogue mismatched socks, and of course holding more baskets inside of baskets . . .

I was a little nervous to make the ask of neighbors (what if they're annoyed?),** but I started a new text strand, leaving out our dear friend Brandi. "Okay! Since we can't physically help, what if we fill this basket up with some self-care? We'll call it the coping mechanism basket. If you have wine, chocolate, bath salts, candles, whatever

---

* Swapping pantries—not to be confused with panties. We're not that kind of neighborhood.

** What a silly thought that I might be annoying my neighbors, when they so joyfully wanted to contribute. I can't believe I almost kept this feeling of contribution and generosity to myself. Never again!

you have on hand—do not run to the store!—set it on your porch tomorrow by noon, and I'll swing by to add it to the basket before I drop it at her door."

The texts came rolling in, *ding ding ding*:

Of course!
Yes, I have wine . . . does anyone know if she likes red or white?
I'm making bath salts with lavender!
I randomly have these fluffy socks and some chocolate!
I'm making banana bread anyway!
I'm swamped, can I contribute to a gift card for dinner with someone?
Me too! I'll grab a DoorDash gift card now.

And so, everyone contributed, and the basket was aggressively full. BrACTSford Place 3:16—I felt like we were living in some sort of Acts church. I set the basket on the doorstep, rang the doorbell, waved into the camera, and zoomed off with a smile. It was like Freezer Friday in a sense: use what you have with who's right in front of you.

Brandi sent us a text almost immediately upon opening her door. "I can't believe I am so lucky to have you all in my life. I'm in tears. This is so special, and I feel so loved. Thank you from the bottom of my heart. This community is unreal."

A month later, another neighbor was facing a really difficult event. I pulled out another basket from my pile and initiated a new text strand. This time, I was more confident. "All right. Time to activate Operation Bradford Basket! You know how to use your powers, ladies! I'll be around tomorrow evening if you want to set something on your porch."

Brandi was the first to respond. "I will use the basket you all gave me last month, and this time, I'd like to drive around and collect the gifts if you don't mind. It would be an honor!"

Generosity never sits still; it keeps going and going. And it often starts with a nervous invitation. At the dinner table, in the front yard, or sometimes a pandemic pivot where the hospitality gets mobile. I learned what a basket can do when my mother opened her doors to guests. I know what dinner can do to break down walls between different beliefs, thanks to my father. Most of all, now I know I am a compilation of the hospitality I learned from my own experiences. I never once thought my mother or father might have been nervous to invite their friends or strangers over. As a child, I just knew what I saw. Now I know it took work, it took intentionality, but they were simply operating in something that came naturally to them with whoever was quite literally right in front of them. They couldn't help themselves. And now I see, I couldn't help using my unique skill of building community and serving others with what I already had: a basket, a frozen pizza, a front yard. Who says God can't take your measly five loaves and two fish and turn it into an epic neighborhood picnic!

> *Generosity never sits still; it keeps going and going.*

Following Your Breadcrumbs

When I think about gifts we were born with, it reminds me that they are simply put there, given, not according to our own efforts. But even with gifts and talents, we still have the command to steward them well. What good is a gift given to you if you never open it? It reminds me of our neighborhood Easter egg hunt. Every year, eggs are hidden, but we don't end up finding them all in the chaos of the excitement, trampoline injuries, and stepping in dog poop. Several weeks ago (mind you, it's June), my son Pruett ran inside screaming like Charlie with a golden ticket in Willy Wonka & the Chocolate Factory. *"I found an egg! It has Skittles! It has a dollar!" It turns out that the egg was there all along in a corner of the yard where no one had bothered to look.*

Sometimes we think we've found all there is to find in the hunt. But it isn't until the chaos settles or maybe the seasons change that we realize we've overlooked an area. There's still a prize to be found!

My treasure map word:
HOSPITALITY

What's your "just-good-at" thing? You might have a couple to brain dump!

Pick one of those items and write about where you think it came from or what has influenced you in this area.

Is there a way in which you could steward your gifts to bring glory to God and show others God's love for them?

seven

Laughable Dreams

My father had a sort of mauve, velvet, overstuffed recliner that I don't recall ever reclining. It only offered repetitive rocking, rhythmic and too fast for relaxation, while he read his Bible or studied (for what, I wasn't sure). Above the recliner hung a framed, pink duck print with a Scripture on it in a very formal, blue calligraphy: "Honor your father and mother . . . *yada yada* . . . and fathers, don't provoke your children to anger." Sometimes I would stare at the little ducks following the big ducks for too long, wondering why they had bonnets on, and forget the task at hand: I was supposed to hold the yellow legal pad with my dad's messy handwriting that I could hardly read and tell him if he'd recited his notes word for word. I said he did, even if I wasn't sure, because I was eight years old and I wanted to go ride my banana seat bike in the cool of the morning before the Texan sun got too hot.

Apparently he was going to the local junior college. Mom said he needed to go to the junior college so he could go to the big law school next. He had to take a lot of tests and one big test that he couldn't mess up. Sounded terrible to my elementary-school brain. *Go to school. Then go to school again? Ew.* As an adult, looking back on the absurdity of my father going to law school makes me wonder what my parents were thinking and how many people must have laughed at such an audacious dream when they were barely making ends meet. My dad (and my mom) had no college degree, and he worked for the local Texas prison system while she stayed home and took care of her plenteous small children.

Did he drop the bomb on Mom out of the blue: "I think I could be a lawyer"? I wasn't invited into that private conversation between my parents, and I wonder if my mom fell out of her chair. Or laughed. Or threw the nearest heavy object in my dad's direction. With six kids and two sets of twins in diapers, did she even have any energy? Regardless, I remember my dad—middle-aged with a classic Protestant mustache—working full-time while going to school full-time and, so the legend is told, acing his college exams. I guess that's what happens when your dreams won't leave you be, and your WHY is bigger than your bank account, life stage, and background.

He would do surprisingly well on the LSAT and get accepted into law school, and my mother would pack up everything we had known in Amarillo, Texas—including Dollface the cat and Jet and Judy (their two beloved Chow Chows)—in a U-Haul, and we'd leave behind our extended family, the neighbors, and our church. We would land in the suburbs of Kansas City, Kansas, to chase Dad's lofty dream. A headline from the *Baker Family Tribunal* might read: "Deranged middle-aged man with seven children (by then their equally crazy mother had one more baby because why not?!) pursues law degree at the elderly age of thirty-eight."

When Dad finished law school, I remember putting on a nice dress for his graduation that my mom had bought for $12.99 off a sale rack. I was in eighth grade, and it was the first time my mom took me to shop at the normal GAP, not GapKids. We didn't have to go to school that day, and I was more excited to skip Spanish II than to see Dad walking across the stage for a formal-looking piece of paper.

When we arrived at the arena, our family took up a whole row, sitting up in the stands while the graduates sat below, proud and smiling. I hadn't noticed until then, but Dad looked a bit old around his young classmates. And he was sitting in the front row closest to the stage. *Maybe it's alphabetical? B for Baker would land him sort of close.*

I leaned over to my mother. "Why does Dad have a different color scarf thingy and the yellow rope tassel?"

She smiled. "Oh, he just did good in school."

"We would like to recognize the top ten in the class at this time. Please stand and offer congratulations to our brightest," the man at the microphone said. My dad stood up, and I was as surprised as everyone.

"Goooooo, Dad!" we hollered.

"And now we would like to recognize our Law Review members . . ." I didn't know what that was, but "reviewing the law" sounded important. Up again he stood.

We all yelped again. "Ya'll see that? Our dad's smarrrrrrt!" I looked over at my mother beaming with a toddler on her lap, my antsy brothers kicking their feet back and forth, and us girls with our new dresses and curled hair. I understood at that moment, at age thirteen, that my father had done something sort of crazy: he believed God put a dream in his heart that was sort of impossible, and he also believed God would make a way for him to accomplish it. Against the odds.

You would think that, with such an ambitious father, academics would have been priority uno in our home when I was growing up. But they weren't really. I went over to my friends' homes and noticed the great emphasis on schooling, homework, and grades. There were consequences for their poor grades: "I can't come over because I got a C in math!" I would look around awkwardly, as I also had a C in math.* But my family wasn't like that. Failing wasn't acceptable, but there was little emphasis on grades or schooling or college.

----

* Why was anyone getting punished for being "average," as the report card clearly stated?

The emphasis was faith, direction, hard work, movement toward the ever-elusive "God's will"—and, of course, *behave for heaven's sake*. I now see how different that way of thinking was, how bent toward God it was. It came uniquely from my father and mother, who didn't have education to lean on. Neither went to college after high school, they weren't hall of fame students, and they came from blue-collar parents. My mother's father owned a junkyard, and my father's father worked in and managed a grain elevator. They probably both got a little caught up in the wrong things along the way, but then they found Jesus and their lives profoundly changed. They knew deeply what many of us might not actually believe: God makes a whole lot of something out of a heap of what appears to be nothing.

My natural leaning, like most kids, was to emulate what I saw from my parents. So in college, at one point, I thought I wanted to go to law school, and for one semester I took pre-law. This included a journalism class in which they wanted me to tell the point of the story in the first three lines. Appalled, I exclaimed in the middle of the class, "What terrible storytelling!"

> God makes a whole lot of something out of a heap of what appears to be nothing.

My professor laughed. "You might be better suited for creative writing, dear." *NONSENSE! I am going to practice the law! Right after I finish this damning opinion piece for the college newspaper on how insanely unafraid college campus squirrels are.*

Now it makes me laugh that I even tried the path of law. I am not book smart. I loathed showing up to class. I wanted to write frivolous stories about squirrels, and I did not want to spend four hours in the law library studying every day when I could be "playing outside." I didn't really feel like I belonged in college, but because I saw my dad do that, and my friends were doing it, I thought maybe I should too. I was trying to copy what I admired, but I was copying the wrong attribute in my father. My dad was never chasing schooling; he was chasing his gifts. School was just the avenue.

After college, I decided maybe I was more like my mom. I delighted in homemaking. It was a place I felt really centered, like I belonged there.* I was having baby after baby, nursing, enjoying hormonal changes, moving, healing from marital tragedy. . . . I was invested in my husband's career, and I enjoyed my choice of staying home and making it a safe and good place for my family. And while I always had side hustles, being a wife and mother was fulfilling for me in that season. Regardless, I still daydreamed of something more. It wasn't that I was dissatisfied or ungrateful, but something in my heart was drawing me toward something else—more of my true self.

I wondered sometimes what it would be like to publish my own thoughts in a real book, but about what I wasn't all that sure. I knew that I liked blogging and sharing funny stories from the weekend, and people were saying I was good at it. Even if I refused to capitalize the beginning of each sentence (some good-girl rebellion).** I knew that I liked to be creative and take pictures or paint or decorate the house on a dime, but could I get paid to do that? Real money, not fun money. I knew how to get scrappy by showing you a before-and-after of a hutch I had painted, but I had bigger aspirations deep down. I had vision and I wanted a business. I didn't want to worry about whether I could buy the frozen bag of cheap chicken at Walmart, or if I needed to put back the milk, or if we'd need our parents to buy baby formula for us that week . . . again. I actually wanted to use all my gifts bundled together to become a millionaire. I'm not exaggerating; I thought about it.*** I was always thinking about

* More than the classroom at least!
** You can thank someone else for all the capitalization and punctuation in here.
*** Please hear the dramatic *Who Wants to Be a Millionaire?* game show music in the background. ME! I want to be that!

91

what it would look like to excel at something and provide more for my family and for others. In big ways.

Women in my circle weren't talking about dreams and aspirations. Most of them seemed completely happy to be stay-at-home mothers. If they needed to work, they simply took up part-time jobs like driving a school bus to make ends meet. "If you could do anything you wanted, what would you do?" I would sometimes ask this, and they would answer, "I'm really happy being at home. I can't even imagine what I would do." End of discussion. Back to discussing making our own baby food or what preschool the kids would attend or how to get these pizza-roll-sized bags out from under our eyes (surely something other than sleep). When I asked men the same question, they had several things they would love to accomplish if they "had their druthers."

My daydreams and aspirations didn't fit in anywhere.

In fact, one time my pastor came over; he knew I blogged. This was before Instagram and TikTok, but I still had several thousand followers. Not huge numbers, but for a mom in Kansas sharing stories and recipes, it was a big deal to me that I could reach so many people outside my immediate community. After dinner, out of the corner of his eye, he saw my computer in the kitchen and walked toward it. "When I was just out of college, I loved to blog," he said. "This was when blogging was filled with great theological discussions. It was mostly dudes, not like it is now. Now it's just so saturated with mommy bloggers and recipes." It flew out of his mouth so casually, so smoothly. He probably didn't notice he had directly bashed what I spent my precious downtime on. Not only did the comment sting, but it also further bolstered the idea that as a woman, I shouldn't be dreaming for more. That I really just needed to stay put in my sweet mama lane . . . forever. There was nowhere else to inspire.

I know it's not like this for everyone, but couldn't it be both? It didn't seem so in my circle, but my dad had done it: parenting and reinventing his life by pursuing his dreams. I had been drawn to starting several businesses: painting appalling name signs with stenciled dogs (I told you it was bad) and walking into a children's boutique and asking if I could sell the atrocities there. They said yes because we both had terrible taste. Two terrible tastes make a right! There was the photography business with embarrassingly over-edited photos (you looked like you were dying of dysentery or you'd just gotten off a cruise ship from the Bahamas).* I have since repented and now only *slightly* edit photos. I worked part-time for our church helping the children's program even though I'd sworn off the ministry. Not only do you get paid peanuts, but people think you only work on Sunday and are happy to let you hold their screaming, pooping, inconsolable babies for two hours while they hear from God. Listen, God is saying, "Cometh back and rescue thine childcare workers from thine offspring."

Like the movies where the alien draws you into their UFO with a light beam you can't look away from, my draw to learn new things, to make money, to be an entrepreneur, and to do business seemed irresistible. I wanted to be on that UFO! So when my friend gave me essential oils and they worked for my family, I decided I would use my voice to talk about them on my blog. Apparently the essential oils business was a network marketing model, something my husband and I had made a pact we would never participate in because we, too, had been the recipients of a "dinner invitation" only to find it was a "unique opportunity" to uncomfortably watch a PowerPoint presentation by a friend of a friend of a friend. And if you think that's a run-on sentence, it is because I am making up for the complete silence in which we finished our meal that night.

But what I had thought was a referral link (a special link that tracks if people purchase a product because of your influence or website), which I had used often to discuss products I liked, turned out to be the very model I had despised.**At this point, I've learned

----

* Forgive me if I ruined your memories one year.
** Funny how God likes to use the things you said you'd never do to humble and shape you.

eating your own words is a delicious part of life and simply gather my fork and knife for all my "I'll-nevers." However, the more I talked about it, the more my customer base grew. I didn't think much of it until I got a bigger paycheck—like bigger than just getting to buy some fun new pants. This was me using my influence to sell a product I like and make actual money. When my husband saw the paycheck, he said, "You have to call them and let them know they made a mistake! That cannot be right!" To which I replied, "No, I think I'm actually working and doing this thing. They're just paying me for my work."

Accidental or not, I found I loved the leadership aspect of helping women sell with integrity, rather than reaching out to their second-grade friends they haven't talked to, well, since second grade, with "a great business opportunity." I also discovered how not to be ashamed to make money, to invest in the community, and to be generous with my products, education, and time. My business grew by leaps and bounds. I was learning just as much as the team I was building was, but that was the magic. I didn't have to have all the answers, but I did need to be able to dream, cast vision, and work hard. Even if others said what I was doing was audacious or foolish or if I didn't quite fit in with my current group of friends. I had daydreamed about this: that I would go to the top of my company, that I would walk across the stage, and that I would get the trophy (and not for the trophy, but for what it meant). I was good at business, selling, making money, providing for my family, and reinvesting back into the community with things that don't need to make a huge profit, like our coffee shop.

Ever since I'd started selling as a kid and walked into the corner store to buy trading cards with my rock-selling money, I daydreamed of having my own little shop. I loved the cash register and the glass case it sat on. I loved that someone knew which buttons to hit and how much change to give (I still cannot do stress math, though, so better to have a calculator on hand). I had never daydreamed of owning a coffee shop; I don't even like coffee. Before you stone me, please know that I do love the smell of coffee, but I am a really big tea snob.* Anyway, the coffee shop is the avenue to have a little store where I can buy and mark up merchandise to make a profit. It employs five people, and we get to participate in community fundraisers and be a pillar in our tiny lake community.

I have also always loved making something better. Every time my mom wanted to wallpaper a new room, I wanted to be right there watching the process and gasping at the *after*. I loved watching my dad build things in the backyard and thinking, *There's no way he's going to pull off this pagoda** in time for my wedding so we can get married under it*. But there it was, and he even added an overbearing water feature. Yes, I have daydreamed about having my own show on TV all about befores and afters. It never gets old! And while I may never get a real TV show—who knows, I'm only forty years old and my father started his career at forty-two—I'm actually ahead of the game! I get to show my transformations on social media to my own audience. I don't do it because I have to or it gets a good response or it grows my influence more. I do it because it's just inside me. It's what I know, and it's just waiting to get out. I truly cannot help it.

Perhaps dreams are not a waste of time at all. The more I live, the more I recognize those as small whispers drawing me toward what's been inside me from the beginning.

---

* Dirt water just isn't my speed.
** What my father called a *pagoda* (which made no sense because I think that's a kind of temple in Asia), we all knew to be a *pergola*, but we never corrected him. He still calls it that seventeen years later.

· · · · · · · · · · *Following Your Breadcrumbs* · · · · · · · · · ·

If you're like me, it's taken a great deal of work to believe that God doesn't just care about you in big ways, but that he cares about you down to how you naturally think and operate, in the minutiae. We like to think of God in these big, ethereal moments when he had Noah build the ark and the flood came—and they were saved! But we don't think about Noah as a carpenter, how he perhaps really loved sanding the rough edges of the hallway corners or how he was excited to map the layout of the cabins to give each family their own space (uhhmm, introverts). Or maybe he liked planning the exact calculations for food on the long trip and he took a couple of casks of wine to make sure they could have a fun party for his wife's birthday?

Well, maybe that's just me. "Dear, did you pack the grass and leaf garland I made for the party decorations?" Once, before a business trip, I laid out a tambourine I had found at the thrift store in the packing pile. My husband said, "I think this is lying here by mistake."

"No, that's for if we accidentally go to another dueling piano bar and it's boring and then I have to do a tambourine solo like last time," I responded in surprise (yes, that really happened, and it was hysterical). I really love making sure people have fun and are entertained!

**My treasure map word:
DREAMER**

What activities do you find yourself drawn to over and over again, as if you just can't help it? Yes, there are items like cooking dinner, going to your job every day, cleaning up after your naughty dog, or the mundane tasks of motherhood—some might feel fulfilling, and some might not. But even inside those activities, even inside what must get done, what can you not help but do even when you're exhausted?

What sparks energy?

Why does it spark energy, and how can you do more of it?

eight

Death by Motherhood

My shirt rolled up like Gus Gus in *Cinderella* as I struggled to get out of the car that July day fifteen years ago. I stroll-waddled my rotund belly into the hospital as contractions hit. My husband and I took the elevator, excitedly smiling at each other. *We're going to be parents. Probably the best the world has ever seen!* Then the pain surged and tightened my belly and reality hit: I would be delivering a watermelon out of a body part that didn't really match the size. I asked for the epidural straightaway. I had a plan, and it was not to feel one more painful contraction.

"We'll need to get you further along, honey," the nurse said. "Trust us. We're not even close."

"How encouraging!" said no one who will soon have a watermelon dropping through the corridors of their most private of parts. She hooked me up to machines and got an IV going. "I'll give you some Pitocin while we wait." Famous last words.

"Listen, I'm sure all pregnant women say this on their first, but my body really, REALLY responds to ANY medicine." She huff-laughed at me. But I meant it. I knew my body. I'm not big on medicine, as in, if you ask me for an ibuprofen, I probably can't find one, and if I do, it's twelve years old and could possibly be a Tic Tac.

I stared at the nurse. She stared at me. I guess I won because she put her gloves on. "Okay, fine. Let's check you, but that's just not typical . . ." She paused and tilted her head.

"Ohhhhhkay. Well, goodness, you are progressing quite well. We will get ahold of your doctor."

"Okay, but can I have the epidural?!" I apparently screamed to no one.

She whispered to the nurse tech, told my husband something, and then left the room.

My husband skulked over. "Babe, there's not enough time for an epidural."

I whimpered. I would need to go ahead and have the baby using my back-up plan—which was to keep the baby inside me. "I cannot have a baby. I don't know how," I cry-whispered to Nato like it was a secret I had been withholding. I didn't have any other plan than a magic carpet ride of an epidural. I didn't read up on breathing techniques or how to push. It sounds idiotic, but keep in mind, I got pregnant on my honeymoon. I'm not much for well-thought-out-and-executed lifestyle choices. But this would lead me to the end of me as I knew it and the beginning of someone else.

He let out a compassionate laugh. I looked at the nurse. "It's not funny, you guys! I don't know what I'm doing! Like really. Gahhhh-hhhd!!!" I said, rolling through another contraction. "Can you call my mom in?"

"Honey, I will tell you exactly what to do," the nurse said. "We will tell you when to push. When you feel that contraction, that means you push."

That seemed simple enough. So I started to push a little on the next contraction. "Ah ah ah! Not yet, young lady!" she exclaimed. "We need to wait for the doctor. Let's hold off for a bit."

Unfortunately, my body was not holding off. If I so much as sneezed, that baby was coming out. My mother stormed in the door.

"Did she just say wait for the doctor? Ridiculous. If you feel like you need to push, you push. We'll deliver this baby if we have to."

"Mom, can you give me a peanut M&M? I'm so hungry!" I yell-whispered as soon as the nurse walked out.

"Of course you are, you're doing such hard work," she said as she dropped one into my mouth, knowing full well I wasn't supposed to eat anything during labor. It was the brown one. *Less dye*, I thought.

Another contraction hit. "I think I'm going to pass out . . . but if the baby comes . . . just wake me up." I noticed my mom was breathing with me, and I remembered she used to be a Lamaze teacher in the '80s. For some reason, I pictured leotard-clad students on giant bouncy balls.

"You're doing amazing. You're going to have this baby." Her sing-song voice lulled me into a calm stupor. I didn't yell. I didn't scream. I didn't get mad at anyone. I resigned myself to the fact that I was dying.*

But I kept being alive. *Oof! I think I'm just going to have to do this . . . deep breath in. Apparently women have done this for thousands of years. If they did it, so can I . . . deep breath out . . . and a little push. Oopsies.*

The nurse came in, and like kids caught cheating on a test, we all acted like I wasn't actively having a baby. Nothing to see here, just . . . there might be a baby under the sheets . . . who's to say . . . ?

Gloves on, she checked me again, and her eyes got big. "It appears you will be having this baby, like, right now. Sara! Get in here! We're crowning!"

No, I'm the one crowning here! You're just sitting there, I thought. *No, don't be mean . . . don't be mean . . . don't be mean.*

They began unplugging and unhooking, and I was looking around confused. Why the hell are we going for a joyride right now? Back

* Soon I would be received into the arms of Jesus, where I could ask him why in the world he made babies arrive out of our nether regions so painfully.

then, you didn't finish labor and delivery in your room. They wheeled you to a birthing room so as to make it the most inconvenient process this side of Missouri. They rolled the bed toward the door and the side of it caught on the door frame with a loud thud. That unhelpful jolt did not encourage me to keep the baby inside. *Keep the baby in. Just keep the baby in.*

"Mrs. Nato, do you mind if we let our students watch your birth? This is a teaching college and . . ."

"I give zero effs; just get this thing out of me!"

The students with their hairnets, blue scrubs, and clipboards lined up shoulder to shoulder around my bed, probably twelve of them. *Why not? I've already lost my dignity, might as well let everyone take a look-see!*

I started pushing. Mom was rubbing my back, saying I was doing a great job. "Chin down. There you go!" My husband was holding my leg, and I could see he was almost crying.

One. More. Push!

They handed me a purple, screaming baby. My husband was cutting the cord, and I was shaking profusely from shock while two of the students were crying. A man with a hairnet popped up from the floor, holding the plug to some machine. I looked through my sprawled legs in stirrups, wondering if he was a hallucination. He exclaimed, "Congratulations!"

Nope, that guy is definitely real.

All 468 of us in that room—the nurses, the students, the doctor who wasn't my doctor (*where is my doctor?!*), my husband, my mother, the machine tech with the hairnet, someone mopping the floor—were feeling all kinds of emotions.

"I'm buying us all cheese pizzas!" I yelled, like I had just climbed Kilimanjaro. "Damn, I'm amazing. I can conquer the world!" They laughed; I laughed. But I didn't immediately feel love for the little human on me like the movies show. I was happy he was here, but I was in shock. Nothing went like I thought it would. I was shaking so hard from the pain.

Apparently they needed to stitch me up, and the students were taking turns learning. Except I could feel the needle.

"Guys, I can feel that. Every stitch."

My mother lost it. "That's enough. Stop and get the doctor in here. She's been through enough already!"

My doctor finally rushed in, with his perfect handlebar mustache and gentle eyes. "Well, my dear, I don't know why I expected anything different from you. Bravo! You have a healthy seven-pound, six-ounce baby!"

"Shouldn't he be bigger? I gained forty-five pounds for heaven's sake!" He muffled a laugh while alternating numbing and stitching.

"Doc, I have a question," I said, while pretending he wasn't sewing me back together. "How long does it take you to get your mustache like that each morning?"

He didn't look up. "About as long as it took you to have this baby. I hear you were quite quick!"

After they wheeled me back (no slamming into the door!) and everyone cleared, Nato fell asleep, my mother went home, and there were no nurses. It was just me and *my* baby. My very own human I'd made. *He's so perfect. The noises he makes. Look at his fingers—why do babies already have long fingernails? Even the pooping is cute. Look at these tiny diapers!* In that moment, there it was: the most immense love for another human. "I just needed a minute. That was all bananas, wasn't it? And you're very cute. I wondered if you would stay purple. But look, everything is fine. You're with Mama," I said in a singsong, high-pitched tone. *What is this voice? Who am I now?*

The thing the baby books don't tell you about leaving the hospital is that two new people emerge. Yes, you're going to come out of there with another person, but you're going to be a different person too. The world changes in the matter of a moment. Some part of me was buried, laid to rest back in that stark, student-filled birthing room. A new person emerged who was intensely immersed in his little toes and the piercing cries, waiting with bated breath to catch the first smile. The feeling of mine-ness and the responsibility were both exhilarating and frightening. And it didn't stop there. Four more babies would come from my body; three would live earthside. Something about making life and nurturing it brought about a new life in me as an individual. Surprisingly though, it also brought a dying of sorts.

> The thing the baby books don't tell you about leaving the hospital is that two new people emerge.

When the second one came, I had a new plan. Now that I'd had one, I knew what to expect. But in truth, it didn't pan out according to the new plan either. She didn't hit her milestones like everyone else. She arrived with stick-straight hair in the air* and in the middle of my marital trauma. She was a delight, but she never crawled. She hopped on her knees across the room, and we laughed it off. "She sure knows how to get across the room!" I simply bought her leg warmers to keep her from tearing up her knees. But language never came, and I started to worry by eighteen months. I became more and more vocal about it. I asked the doctor, and he said her big brother was just doing all the talking for her. But that didn't explain it.

As time passed and nothing changed, I sought an ENT doctor on my own with no referral, which is apparently a little difficult. I didn't know then, but from that point, I was learning advocacy for her. The ENT looked at me with a sigh after she checked her ears. "Well, this makes sense; she cannot hear. Luckily, it can be fixed. Anatomically, she has a part of her ear that isn't draining, and it's as if she is underwater listening to us. Well, more like under tar."

I could handle this. It's just tubes. They assured me she'd start talking once she could hear. But months passed, and little progress was made. At two and a half, she was falling so far behind her peers in labeling animals and noises that I became worried. She refused to potty train, and I couldn't get her in any preschools. So now I had no real answers, a child who didn't speak, and a doctor telling

* Like those troll dolls from the '90s.

me it was nothing to worry about. My gut wouldn't let it go. The state educational program denied me because she wasn't "disabled enough." I was stuck. I prayed and prayed for answers and wisdom, but I couldn't help but feel so alone and unsure.

I knew from my education background that early intervention is extremely important. So when she was three or four, I googled my brains out and called two children's hospitals to get her evaluated. They both had nine- to twelve-month waiting lists. *This can't be how it is! Where's the instruction manual? Where's the guide on what path to take when you know something isn't okay with your child and you might lose your mind if no one helps you?* I finally asked my Facebook friends, and lo and behold, there appeared like a northern star a nurse who mentioned a developmental preschool.

I called immediately. They were full. Of course I couldn't help but burst into tears. Exhaustion often doesn't accompany dignity, and I babbled, "I just don't know what else to do. No one will listen to me." On the other end, the woman sighed with compassion. "You know what, why don't you bring her in and let me take a look? I can at least evaluate her."

I cried again, this time in relief. In the waiting room, I stared at the other mothers and fathers and the few siblings who peppered the space. I knew it was rude to ask what was going on with their children, but I wondered silently. Through the windows, I could see the most magnificent indoor playground with a swirly slide. A track and tricycles surrounded it. A child was learning to pedal as a nurse in scrubs was gently putting a foot back on the pedal. *See! Push! You're moving!*

When the nurse arrived in the waiting room, she motioned for me to come back. She took her job seriously but also had a cheery disposition, and I immediately liked her. "We spoke on the phone. I'm CeCe. Lila is a real joy. Her tutu is so fun!" she said as she slid a paper across the table. "Now, here is the evaluation we just did, and you are right. She is very delayed. I can't believe no one is helping you! Speech is here . . . should be here. Motor skills are here but should be here. . . ." On and on.

I tried not to cry from the sheer validation *and* the disappointment that I was indeed right all along. She noticed my watering eyes. "I know this is so hard. No one tells you how to do this. Anyway, I'm going to talk to my supervisor to see if we can make room. We're going to get that girl the help she needs!"

"God has sent us an angel with Mrs. CeCe, Lila," I said with a smile. Lila cheered, "CeCe!" She had few words, but that name rolled off her tongue quite well. Later that year, I asked Lila who she wanted to be for Halloween, and she said CeCe. So I put Lila in scrubs and glasses with a name tag. When I told CeCe about it, CeCe said she would dress like Lila and wore a tutu and ridiculous tights. What we didn't know was that CeCe's mother had died the previous Halloween, and she was really struggling. Later she told us how Lila was the joy she needed to get through that devastating day. It looks one-way, but sometimes by helping others, we get help too. That school became our safe place. I was heard, we weren't the odd ones, our child was loved, and we were all fighting a really hard thing.

Lila made great leaps in her motor skills, speech, and emotional milestones. We had her genes tested to no avail and ended up finding a neurologist to make her official diagnosis: "She's quite honestly a mystery, and I am slow to put labels on children because they linger quite long even if untrue. But she is severely developmentally delayed with apraxia [difficulty with skilled movements, such as the motor skills of the mouth, tongue, and voice] among other various deficiencies. We don't know how it will be for her in the future; she most likely will not read or live alone fully independently." He said this gently, and we received it. I went home and put her down for a nap and laid down my dreams for who I thought she would become too. I shut the door and wept.

Another thing those baby books don't tell you is what happens when dreams die. What the process is like. What the grief is like. *She won't get married; she won't become a teacher or a doctor.* Yet, as time went by, the acceptance and the gratefulness arrived. How unnecessary it became to change my children and how it freed me up to simply love them for exactly who they are. How they will surprise me. How they will be a doctor who fixes my broken perspective and gives me a new and better prescription. And how they will be a teacher who teaches me a better way to love and accept and dream.

Against all odds, in the third grade, Lila started reading words. And in the fourth grade, she wrote her own story using pictures above each word that she could read.* Now in seventh grade, she reads and copies books for fun. *For fun!* She makes friends easily and starts conversations with our adult neighbors, looking them in the eye with genuine curiosity. "And how was your day, Sara?"

> *It became unnecessary to change my children and it freed me up to simply love them for exactly who they are.*

We laugh regularly at her antics. She has an intense laundry obsession. If you accidentally drop a sock, she sneaks behind and grabs it for the wash pile. *Has anyone seen my other sock?!* Lila looks away gingerly. She will wash one towel at a time and shrink your best pants in the blink of an eye. I can't tell you how many times we've run to the dryer only to see our nicest wool sweaters morphed into great pieces of fashion for the Barbie dolls. But we just can't be mad at her for it; she is full of purpose and joy.

Every day I look at her and thank God for giving her to us, even though I don't know what I'm doing. But she has taught me what my oldest has as well: how to love and that, while one part of you dies (the old you), another part begins to live. There is always life in death. Often through death.

When things feel difficult, I like to tell my children, "There's only one way through this, and it's through." I can't explain to them the rest of what I know because the time will come when they'll have to learn it for themselves: the way through this valley, in between the mountains, is what will shape you the most. It's where I've changed

....

* I cried listening.

the most. It's where I find God's presence nearest and where I find my greatest rewards. And it's where you'll find a cemetery of old Jamis. I've buried the past versions of myself, the expectations I had of me, and all the things I knew for sure. I sometimes visit the gravestones and rub my fingers across the dates. *I remember her; I remember that.* It would be sad, except what arose from those graves is the person I was always meant to become who is here now holding these flowers.

Following Your Breadcrumbs

Sometimes it's hard for us to think we won't always have all the answers. There's a certain mirage of safety when you know the "right answer" all the time with no wiggle room, especially about yourself. When I was in high school and college, I felt very certain about most things. Everything was black-and-white or this-or-that. As I've experienced life, traveled out of the country, and faced my own suffering, I've discovered an untidy nuance of being a human: things aren't always so simple or so hard and fast. It's not either-or, but a lot of and. I can believe this way, and I can understand why someone might see it differently. As soon as I give myself the freedom not to have all the answers and to keep learning, which includes quite a bit of unlearning, I get one step closer to finding the real me. Rethinking the "right answers" or undoing your expectations actually opens you to discovering more of who you're meant to be, but it means opening your eyes to seeing something differently.

My treasure map word:
PIONEER, MOTHER

In what ways have you had to bury past expectations or versions of yourself in order to see new life appear?

What situations do you find yourself in now that aren't going as you planned? How might those be leading you toward a death that could bring life?

Have you had to bury a past dream only to find a better one was created?

If so, describe what those figurative burials taught you or how they changed you to become the person you are today.

nine

Someone Else's Garden

My father had a peach tree in the backyard when I was a child. I quickly lost interest in it after he concocted a peach-and-raw-egg smoothie and made each of us taste it. He relented once I gagged, but it's no surprise that I find peach-related products revolting to this day and launch an all-out peach smear campaign anytime someone brings peach pie to a picnic. "Gross. They're furry, people!"

What most captivated my attention in the yard was my mother's rather large garden. She planted it out front inside the white picket fence that kept her unruly children in. For hours, she hunched over in the sun with a hat, weeding and keeping up, hands in the cool soil. My mother was a mystery to me. I stared at her from the large living room window in the cool air-conditioning and wondered why she spent so much time away from us children out there. She wasn't known for being particularly outdoorsy. She liked the inside things of life. But there she was, transplanting lamb's ears from one area to the other. "See, it's taking over this area. These plants are going to crowd out the others," she explained. "Feel this leaf; that's why it's called lamb's ear." She was right. I wanted to lie in it and take a nap immediately. She let me collect the seeds from her colorful zinnias, which were hard and pea-sized, indestructible. If I couldn't sell them, I would replant them elsewhere in the neighborhood.

I chose Mr. Baggott's yard because the myth was that he was old or dead or a recluse, and I imagined he needed something colorful in his very brown and grassless backyard.* While working, I waved to the windows in case he was watching. Maybe he smiled; maybe he growled. Either way, he certainly didn't stop me if he was there. Anyway, why would someone stop a precocious girl from making a mythical, possibly dead man's life more entertaining and beautiful? I recruited a couple of neighbors and siblings as usual, and we spent the better part of several days planting seeds with no instruction. I can't tell you how it turned out because I never watered them or checked on them again. I figured nature would "do its thing" and take care of my hard work. It was my first garden in someone else's yard.

When my family moved from Texas, my mother took a giant paper bag of seeds she and I had picked the season before and planted them at our new house in Kansas. The flower garden was not as large, but the zinnias lined the driveway magnificently in contrast to the suburban, beige homes. At the Kansas house with more yard, Dad decided he needed tomatoes and peppers of all kinds. Off he went, constructing a tall fence and an unruly garden. We were all thankful it was hidden on the back side of the house. Then he planted apricot trees in the front and several apple trees in the back. He didn't do much weeding, just planted and watered and trusted nature would provide most of what the plants needed. Every summer after that, Mom would make homemade salsa. Everyone raved about it. Anyone who visited went home with three tomatoes or twenty-five peppers. "Watch out for that red one! It is as hot in as it is out!" Dad would yell as they left.

Mom also did the tedious task of making and canning apricot jelly. "This is a labor of love for your father. You know how he feels

* Have you noticed how many other people's yards I spent time in as a child?

112

about apricots."* I did know, because we had to hear about it at most dinners when he moaned with delight, slathering butter and the jelly on a roll and gingerly placing it in his mouth. *My word, Dad. Get a room.* My mother smiled in accomplishment. We nodded in approval but went for the knock-off grape jelly from a squeezy tube that made a fart noise.

Even though my dad bragged about how Mom made the jelly just for him, we all knew nothing ever stayed put in the pantry. "Now go bring this apple butter to the neighbors." The garden was never just for us; it was for everyone else.**

Once I had a home of my own, I had no real interest in gardening at all. I was knee-deep in trauma, a toddler and a newborn, home projects, and just trying to keep up. My father-in-law planted hostas for us because our front yard was so barren, looked terrible, and we just couldn't afford plants. He also put in red mulch (RED MULCH!). I gasped in horror when I walked half naked past the front window to see him and his brother unloading sacks of unnatural wooden chips the color of Satan. I immediately fell to the floor and crawled back to the bedroom.

I called my husband immediately. "Your dad can't just come over whenever he wants, unannounced, and plant things in OUR yard. . . . Also, I have very little on! And the mulch . . . it might as well be neon!"

He was laughing. "I didn't know he was coming over. Listen, he's just being nice. He's planting a garden for you. And are you still naked . . . ? I can be home in fifteen!"

You could almost hear my eye roll. "I don't want someone else's garden. I can make my own!"

> *The garden was never just for us; it was for everyone else.*

---

* Aren't apricots the annoying little cousins to peaches?
** To this day, I still get apple butter in my Christmas stocking.

Surprisingly, my father-in-law discontinued red mulch and un-announced visits after that. We drove by that old house last year, and most of the hostas were still there two owners later, but they were even bigger. It made me smile. A part of our memories still lived there; now someone else gets to enjoy them.

"They have no clue what I endured for those hostas!" I looked over at Nato as we laughed. He added, "Why don't you strip down and run through the yard for old times' sake?"

When we moved to our next house, it was still winter. The trees and yard looked pretty barren. As we painted and worked on the interior to make it our own, spring suddenly sprung, and the most beautiful bush of flowers popped up on the side of the house. This is the magic of moving in winter: previous owners will hardly tell you if they get water in the basement, let alone give you the rundown of plant life you'll find come spring. I clipped them and brought them inside, surprised when I found tiny ants crawling all over them. I googled how to get rid of the ants. I discovered the flower was called a peony and that the peonies and ants have a mutual relationship. The flower provides food for them, and the ants protect them from other insects. I looked forward to the bush blooming every year, ants and all. I thanked God for whoever decided to plant peonies without me in mind. Yet there I was standing over them gasping with delight every spring.

Four years later, on the next move, I lamented. This was the hard move, the one we didn't want to make but felt called to. I was grieved, but I knew it was right; I knew God wouldn't lead us astray, but that didn't make it any easier when we were in the middle of it. I wanted to bring that peony bush with me, but they're finicky, so I didn't risk it. Instead, I pictured the new homeowner gasping like I did when spring arrived. *It must stay. She belongs there.*

We moved in the heat of the summer to the suburbs, and I was so pregnant with my fourth that there was no time to plant a garden. The grass was green, but I couldn't tell what would come up in the yard, nor did I look very hard. I was exhausted with four kids, and we lived like hermits through the fall and winter. As the weather was getting nicer, I noticed a long line of plants popping up against the house. At first, I thought they were weeds. Then one day when the plants got tall enough to flower, I noticed the first round bud. I screamed, "They're peonies! There are five peony bushes back here!" I cried.* It was like God was meeting me right there in kindness that he didn't have to show. I left one bush; he gave me five back. My daughter Penelope picked one and brought it to me. "Oh no! Ants!"

"The ants protect the plant. They don't want to hurt you, baby."

And maybe this lesson on ants and the peony was preparing me for what was to come.

As our third summer in the suburbs approached and the peonies died, I felt inexplicably drawn to have a garden with tomatoes and peppers. The inexplicable part was that we had decided it was time to move again. A unique, historic house with five acres had come on the market. It felt like we were driving onto a *Pride and Prejudice* set. The owner was an avid gardener, and a giant magnolia tree shaded part of the backyard. We felt like we had to jump. And jump we did. We got our house ready to sell, and we had an architect make plans for renovations and additions to the new house at great expense. We were all-in on this dream.

Even in the chaos of babies and toddlers and architects, cleaning out, throwing away, prepping, and primping, I kept feeling drawn to plant a garden in the yard of a home we were selling. I couldn't put the thought away. *Why do you care about making a garden for people you don't even know? You won't even get to have the tomatoes!* My husband agreed. This was so silly.

But the next day I was at the garden store buying all the supplies, and he was tilling the ground and making me a garden box. Suddenly, I understood what my mother and father understood: the process is as important as the yield. The garden is where you go to weed things

---

* I actually cried.

out, physically through the dirt, and through your life.* I just had to do it. Moving was stressful enough, and I'd need somewhere to say goodbye. That six-by-three-foot box is where I buried my emotions. Plus, it would be my parting gift to the new owners. Everyone loves fresh tomatoes or salsa—and if they don't, they don't belong on this street as they're likely serial killers.

That summer, we sold the house—four times. And four times it fell through by some odd means. At the end of the day, we kept not agreeing to meet the demands of the buyers who wanted it. They had no clue they were getting the amazing hardwood floors we installed and all the fantastic renovations—and the best neighbors, the dinner club of twenty years, the block parties, and a damn salsa garden! *We should buy this house . . . oh, wait, it's already ours. What are we thinking?!*

By the fifth go at putting it back on the market, I looked at my husband and said, "I think God is just saying NO."

So that summer, we ate from and enjoyed what was intended to be someone else's garden. I sometimes would choke up picking the tomatoes, thanking my past self for planting it anyway. For being foolish enough to believe that planting a garden is good even if you don't get to reap from it. Even if you have to leave it behind, and even if your tears watered it. Someone will benefit from it, even if that someone isn't you.

Our next big house project came to us by miraculous means—as if God held a house for us, waiting for the perfect time. We wouldn't have had the means to buy that home when it was put on the market. It sat for us, while we got ready, while God said no to other things. (This was the lake house.) To the side of the driveway sat a giant, I mean colossal, magnolia tree. I remembered the historic home with its big magnolia that we had to give up and felt a tiny pang of loss still. Behind the magnolia at the lake house were three

* If there were a candle scented like fresh dirt mixed with tomato leaves and a touch of sunscreen, I would be the first in line.

116

ghastly-looking bushes that I decided we'd take out one day, but as usual we had too many projects going on inside for now.

As spring arrived, we went to a friend's house for dinner like we often did. As soon as we got out of the car, the most gorgeous, pungent floral odor hit my nostrils: lilacs! I asked if I could take some home and she cut some right then and there. I turned to my husband and said, "Nato, let's put lilac bushes under that garage area where those awful bushes are. Three, right under the windows." I peppered my friend with questions: *Are they hard to keep? When do you plant them?* Shoot, I had missed the chance to plant them during the colder part of spring; the next opportunity would be the cool of fall.

The next day, I went out to the lake house to check on a project. When I opened my car door, I looked around frantically. Speaking to no one, I said, "Who has lilacs around here?!" I looked to my neighbor's house on the left—nothing. And then to the right—nope. Behind the magnolia were exactly three blooming lilac bushes. I ducked under the tree and ran my hands across the flowering stems as if to make myself believe this was real. *Either the Lord loves me so much that he replaced the mangy bushes with lilacs in the middle of the night or, more realistically, the woman who lived here before planted them.* The only things I knew about this woman were that she had died suddenly and that this was her dream home. She had planned to live out her days there with her second husband. But when she died, the house went to the children, who never used it. After several years and many realtors, they got tired of holding it and sold it to us for less than it was worth. To us! So here I stood, undeserving, holding the lilacs she planted. Putting them in vases all around the house. She is a part of these bushes—and a part of my story now.

We are all living in someone else's garden. Another woman came before us and softened the soil and planted the seeds. We might find ourselves with our mother's hands or our grandmother's knack for keeping peace. We might have a habit of splurging on the quality things like our aunt or finding over-the-top joy in every holiday like our second-grade teacher. We might find ourselves incredibly welcoming like our mother-in-law or prone to open our doors like our neighbor friend. Women who have come before us may be gone now, but we pick up their work gloves or their shovel and continue on, not as if they weren't here anymore but with gratitude that they were here, just as I am. It makes me tender toward the ones who will pick up my gloves someday. I want to pass my shears with dirt on my face and say, "I did my best for you. I didn't just take what was mine. There's hope for you in this soil. I sowed seeds of joy for you."

> *We are all living in someone else's garden.*

Following Your Breadcrumbs

I have a friend who, whenever she hears live music, is drawn to it like a mosquito to one of those aggressively loud bug zappers you can buy at Costco. She literally cannot help herself when she hears the music. Her head turns, she gives no warning of getting up, and you'll find her swaying and singing along, raising her Michelob ULTRA to the band.

On one recent trip, we went to a bar known for their live music. It was getting late, and I was getting tired. "Hey, I am going to the bathroom!" I excused myself but then accidentally walked out the door. As I left, I turned around to see her beaming, yell-singing, and it made me smile. I walked the mile to the hotel, got in my pajamas, read my latest fiction book, then went to bed. Her joy=live music. My joy=stories. We are magnets to our loves. Yet often we confuse things that have always brought us small joys with "coincidences." They are so much more than that.

I get to enjoy the tomatoes, the magnolia, and the lilacs because someone planted them—and when they did, God had me in mind. He is after our joy and our smile more than we're willing to believe.

My treasure map word:
SOWER

Name small pleasures, smiles, or joys you've encountered these past couple of years, or list the activities that have always brought you joy.

Where did those things come from, as in whose work or toil made it possible for you to enjoy these things? Who left something behind for your pleasure?

Have you ever seen those things as simply a gift meant for you? Do you see a connection between those and your purpose or roles where you thrive?

ten

Blind Driving 101

F ive kids lived next door to us on Monroe Street. Jordan was my
age, and we kissed behind the old, brown, rusted-out Toy#ta
truck.* We were married several times by age eight, and we outfitted
our home with the latest tree-house fashions of the time (a random
carpet tile, Mother's nice pillows, candy cigarettes, nutty bar wrap-
pers, etc.). Mostly, we tore up and down the street on our banana
seat bikes until our mothers called us in for dinner. Sometimes I
would eat dinner at Jordan's house if Caroline, his mother, let me.
Caroline liked me because I was quirky, unkempt, and made her
laugh, which I was glad for on Friday nights because that's when
she made homemade pizza.

Our mothers, at one time, were best friends. They both gardened,
they did puppet shows at kids' church together, and they played
cards and drank wine coolers on Friday nights while we slept (or
pretended to). They were also pregnant at the same time in 1986. My
mother had twins, Audrey and Andrew, and Caroline had Hannah.
But something went wrong in the womb or at birth, and Hannah

---

* It was missing an o after a dare.

would be severely disabled, unable to speak or move on her own for the rest of her life. No one said anything directly about her differences, but as the twins grew, so did the disparities between them and Hannah. The twins were saying cute sentences, and Hannah would make strange noises looking up to the sky. The twins were running, and Hannah sat in her chair that we called "the bucket." She was moved out of it for bathing or sleeping—or when we put her in the horse trough where we spent the summer swimming. We didn't ask for permission. She was watching us swim and smiling. Her sister had the grand idea to take Hannah out of the bucket and hold her while Jordan, the others, and I created a whirlpool. We had done that often—running together in the same direction as fast as we could to make a homemade whirlpool—though never with Hannah. We thought she was missing out. Run, get caught up in the whirlpool, ride the magnificent Midwestern horse trough waves, repeat. Adrianne held her tightly.

Hannah laughed and laughed, high-pitched, wheezing with joy, which made us all laugh. We did that for a while until Caroline came out and said she would "whoop our asses" if we ever did that again. We all rolled our eyes. *Fun killer.* We did it again the next summer when Caroline was away running errands.

"Hannah, don't you dare tell your mama!" I whispered, laughing at my own joke while unbuckling her. We decided not to put Hannah on the zip line that reached from the garage roof to the light pole in the alley because the bucket was too cumbersome and heavy (thankfully). But she could still watch us, laugh, and, more important, remain alive.

That was just how it was. Hannah was differently abled, but we just made her part of our world. We didn't know to think any differently about her, yet she was creating a soft spot inside me. One that I would need later for an unexpected hardship on my own journey. We pushed Hannah on walks, bumping into each uneven part of the janky sidewalk. We begrudgingly watched *Barney* episodes with her when she got upset—that annoying purple dinosaur immediately soothed her. Hannah came to the park, and we put her on the merry-go-round. Hannah came to the pool and sat in the shade and sweat, so we would bring over cups of water to sprinkle her. Hannah was at every birthday party, and we went to Hannah's birthday party and blew out her candles for her. She couldn't say one word, but she could laugh. Hannah taught us joy and that there was joy in others' joy and in just being. There was nothing required of us to make Hannah love us; we simply had to be there. We just had to open the doors and push her through. Our presence was what she wanted, and as kids, that's all we could give her anyway.*

When my dad decided casually that he should go to law school, we moved away from Monroe Street, the delights of the horse trough, and sweet Hannah to the middle-of-nowhere Kansas. My dad was a nontraditional student (i.e., older than everyone), and non-trads are really annoying because they are actually in school with a de-termined purpose, so they sit in the front row to prove it. My father immediately found Clay, also in the front row. But Clay had to sit there because he was hard of hearing. He was also blind.

Clay would forget he was wearing headphones to help him hear the professor and talk loudly to my father, thinking he was whisper-ing. "My gas is horrible today."

"We know; the whole class knows," Dad would say with a cringe. He could hear snickering from the rows behind them. Clay and Dad became friends, and Dad volunteered to help Clay study, as it came with perks like their own study room, which was a hot commodity.

Clay regularly called our house and spoke to everyone available. For hours. We all had to take turns, and if we didn't want to, we had better find something to do that was worthy of avoiding a forty-five-minute conversation on obscure World War II facts** or the science behind cats living nine lives (he also talked to my cat Dollface at

---

* Besides a mild heart attack in the whirlpool.
** Actually helpful if you had a report due—there was no Google!

123

length) or why peaches have fur (he knew I hated them and was concerned).

"Clay, what was happening in August 1981 when I was born?" I asked him once.

No pause at all. "August. 1981. That, that . . . that was when . . . that was when . . ." I could hear him rocking back and forth and flapping his hands a little. "Reagan was president. He was an actor, isn't that crazy? MTV started. You like MTV? It used to be actual music videos nonstop, no shows. No reality TV. I'm not against that, but I do wish they had more music. Isn't that strange? It's called music TV . . . but there's not a lot of music anymore. We also reached Saturn on the *Voyager*. Saturn has sixty-two moons! . . ." This is when I would set down the telephone and do my homework or wrangle a sibling to chat. "Listen, it's your turn. I have to organize my Beanie Babies collection."

Some days, Dad brought Clay home from school for dinner, smelling like stale cigarettes. Clay called everyone by their pet names: Dad was Jet (one of the Chow Chows we had at the time), Mom was Queen, I was Dollface (like my cat). He often said he had to go talk to Jet (the dog) and always came back inside smelling like fresh smoke. He rocked back and forth and exclaimed that "Judy" was the best cook. "Clay, I put some apricot jelly on this roll Terri made. Try it," my father would say as he slathered up a hot roll like it was a party trick.

"Dammit, this apricot jelly is the best! Jet, you were right. Sh—, sorry, I know you all don't cuss here."

At the end of one such dinner, Dad decided we should take Clay for a ride on the John Deere buggy we drove frequently to our uncle's house two miles away. It had a bucket that would lift so you could dump dirt in and out. It could also hold about four small humans. Clay sat next to me, and I drove on rabbit speed, as fast as it could go up the street. He loved it; he was satisfied. But Dad wasn't. When we got back, Dad said Clay should drive.

I looked at him with big eyes. "Dad, he can't drive; he's blind!"

Clay laughed. "Dollface! What?! I'm blind?"

"What you'll have to do is put it on turtle speed. Jami, you're on tapping duty. You sit next to him and tap him on the shoulder he needs to turn toward when he's going too far to the right or left," Dad explained. "Clay, this is the gas and the brake. You're going to have to be gentler than you think. Okay, try it, I'll walk next to you."

Jerking forward and backward, begging for a chiropractic visit, we were laughing hysterically until, eventually, Clay got the hang of it and it became a little smoother. Suddenly, my dad was jogging. My dad does not jog, so that in itself was entertaining. I was tapping Clay's shoulders. Clay was steering well, actually.

"Okay, move it a little faster . . . toward rabbit." And then Dad was shrinking in the background. Clay was scream-laughing, high-pitched, rocking back and forth and stringing together expletives I had never thought to combine.

"I'm driving! I'm driving a convertible! This is illegal! My glass eyeball is going to fall out!"

My siblings were in the back bucket, cheering, "You're driving, Clay! You're going to get arrested! The police are coming!"

We laughed so hard that I thought I might choke. The wind was blowing through his hair, he was squealing, and the sun was setting in the most perfect pinks. I wanted to point out the sky to him but caught myself. *He can't see that.* But he didn't need to. You'd have thought we were on a NASCAR track or on the *Voyager* to Saturn in 1981, but we were going ten miles an hour in Stilwell, Kansas.

Clay may have been limited in some areas, but what he lacked in sight, he experienced tenfold in all the other senses. When I saw his joy, I wondered what God must be like. What limited joy I had experienced because I took most of life for granted. His joy was uncomplicated, unattached, stripped down until it was pure. I am sure I got a glimpse of heaven—and it wasn't even through my own joy; I was just watching his.

I think about Hannah and Clay* a lot when I try to navigate life with our Lila. In a way, they prepared me for this time when I feel like I'm doing a bit of blind driving myself. I wonder if we're tapping too far right or veering too far left on the road, but thinking about Hannah and Clay reminds me how simple and joyful it is to love Lila. She requires less than most and is happy when others are happiest. She regularly has laugh attacks in church.** She cried with tears of joy when her sister Penelope got a bike for Christmas. She killed a lightning bug trying to hug it. But I also think about those around Lila—the kids in the neighborhood and her siblings—and how they are being shaped to see those who are differently abled and to find ways to include them. As I was shaped by how God made a way for me to experience Hannah and Clay to provide for my own journey ahead. It's not something you can teach someone. Saying "Make sure you include people who don't have a place" can make you aware, but it doesn't make a soft spot or change a heart. Being with someone who doesn't have a seat, and moving in compassion to make room for them, does.

A mother faces a lot of fears when she finds out her child will not be like the other children. God gently clued me in through Hannah and Clay. My greatest fear goes something like this: *No one will love her, really love her, like she deserves. No one will be her friend. She's not going to be included. It's cute now because everyone accepts a child, but what about when she's a teen or an adult?* I regularly need God to show me that the same grace that is sufficient for me is sufficient for Lila. And the same provision he gives to me, he gives to her. I often get lost thinking God won't take care of Lila, and

---

* Clay never used his law degree, but he did graduate with honors along with Dad. Clay teaches history and debate at a local college, has quit smoking, changed his eating habits, and the report is that his gas is much more palatable.

** Honestly, I don't know where she gets that.

he often proves me wrong. Like the time I went on a field trip with Lila's class.*

I signed up for the trip because this was the one on economics. They were going to make products, set up a store, and sell to their peers. In the end, they'd see who made the most money. My little entrepreneurial heart leapt to volunteer. The kids received their instructions, and we helped them set up their products. Lila's group was selling chicken nuggets and bracelets. The bracelet-making was too complicated, so Lila stole nuggets when no one was looking. For the most part, Lila had a great time and was included. But I was making sure of it, and maybe the other parents were too. It is sometimes uncomfortable to see Lila with her peers because the developmental chasm is so much more apparent, like when Hannah was next to the twins. I could feel my anxiety rising, like the smell of burned brownies at the shop next to us. *I just want her to be loved and included.* She joyfully inserted herself in the middle of the marketing chaos, yelling, "Buy one, get one free!" mimicking her peers.

> *I often get lost thinking God won't take care of Lila, and he often proves me wrong.*

When the event was over, I was exhausted from my inner turmoil, but she seemed pretty energetic and unaware. (A superpower of mothers is hiding all the emotional and mental tornadoes that threaten to demolish a child's good time.) I got stuck cleaning up the table while the kids went to the main room to hear the results: how much they made, who made the least, which team won . . . *Gosh, this is brutal! But it is real life.* I thought of the coffee shop we owned and its slumps and high seasons. But I mostly thought

----

* I don't like to go on field trips with my kids because they give me social anxiety. But I understand the importance of trying so your kids can look back and say, "My mom was a huge weirdo and embarrassed me a lot, but she showed up."

of Lila working behind the counter one day and it made me smile. *We can provide her a job.*

When I finished daydream-cleaning, I couldn't find Lila. I scanned the room in a panic for several minutes (probably only five seconds). I saw girls from her group, and in the background standing outside the circle, I finally saw Lila, unsure of where to sit in the huge mob of kids. She couldn't see me or hear me. My heart broke.

It reminded me of a day when I had dropped something off at her old school and her class was in gym, which I happened to walk by on my way out. I peered through the window and looked for Lila. She was in the corner by herself, holding a ball while her peers played without her.

Good thing I'm here. I waved my hand and started to maneuver through the children toward her.

Then to the left, I heard a little mouse voice. "Liiiiiila!"

Lila turned and beamed. "Francie!" Lila moved toward the little girl who was making a space. "Sit here. Crisscross, like me." I moved quietly back to the back. I tried really hard to pretend like my allergies or a mixture of prepubescent BO with a touch of boiled hot dog had gotten to my eyeballs. It's one thing to doubt God's provision, but it's another thing for his tender and compassionate provision to meet you smack-dab in the middle of your doubt. I knew right then what God was doing: he was simultaneously providing for Lila and for me. He made a friend make room for Lila; he made room in my heart to believe that he goes before her. He will make a way for her, and—news flash!—it won't always be through me. Perhaps he had created the chaos that day to keep her from seeing or hearing me and then provided Lila's own tapper on her figurative buggy. All so he could show me more of himself, to let heaven come down and say, *I'm making a way that you couldn't anticipate. I made others with the same soft spot.*

We all need the Francies in our lives—and more than that, we need to believe that God will provide them for us and for those we love the most.

When my son Layne was on a baseball team, he befriended a boy named Patrick.* I could see them slapping each other on the field, laughing as little boys do. When I met Patrick's parents for the first time, I noticed how attentive they were to Lila—asking questions, listening with curiosity, and laughing with her. It's not normally like that. Understandably, most people don't know how to treat differently abled humans, let alone differently abled, awkward preteens. I hadn't met their son yet, but as they came off the field, I congratulated him. "You cracked that ball right down the middle!" He didn't respond and looked away, not because he didn't want to, but nothing came out. I saw then that he was also differently abled.

Patrick was ridden with seizures, and they started to get worse with no reason. When he was hospitalized after a particularly terrifying event, I had to tell Layne we would have to reschedule their playdate. Layne wanted to know why.

"Well, you know he has some special needs kinda like Lila; he's having these seizures, and it's scary. The doctors are trying to figure it out, but he needs to rest."

Layne looked up immediately, his brows furrowed in confusion. "Patrick does not have special needs. AT ALL. I would know; we're like best friends." My eyes stung with the start of tears. He only saw Patrick as his friend.

We do a lot of things wrong in this family, but we all have the same God-shaped soft spot. We've had to watch someone we love being rejected or not included because they are different. If you watch that enough, it starts to irritate you, then it gives way to compassion. I remember praying that Hannah would be healed. *Why don't you let her walk, God?* And then with Lila, I tried to fix her with potions and pills and surgeries. But God knit their DNA like this; they, too, were made on purpose and for a purpose. Just because

---

* Coincidentally, my husband went to high school with his father, and they would sit in the stands and make fun of each other's bad hair choices and puka shell necklaces.

someone can't speak or hear or see or function like we do doesn't mean they're any less valuable. The softness deepens over time and changes our minds, freeing us to simply enjoy them, love them, and learn something about God that we didn't know yet.

At some point, we simply start making a way and pulling out a chair for those who can't pull it out for themselves. And then we stop expecting everyone to fit into our small framework of what it's like to be a part of this diverse human population. We simply accept and include. Sometimes we do it on purpose; sometimes we don't. But God's provision remains the same. He gives the neighbors, the classmates, the teammates—the ones with a similar soft spot—to come alongside. Their presence says, *You're human and you're worthy. I want to be with you just the way you are. You were made on purpose to show us a part of God we couldn't understand without you.*

Following Your Breadcrumbs

The breadcrumb for this can be found in what makes you feel deep sadness, particular softness, profound joy, and even anger. I heard pastor Rich Villodas put it simply: "What makes you mad, sad, anxious, and glad?" Those feelings help us pinpoint where we empathize the most with ourselves and others. Often, they developed because of some early or recurring experiences you've had or even a fresher trauma from the tumultuous past couple of years. It's time to pay attention to those feelings, however uncomfortable they may be.

My treasure map word:
DIFFERENTLY ABLED

What's your unique soft spot, and where did it come from?

What has shaped this empathy?

How has God provided tenderly for you or someone you love in a way that has shaped you?

What causes do you support? Where do you volunteer time and donate money? Where do you find yourself tender NOW? What makes your heart glad when you spend time there?

Have you ever looked back to see how God might have prepared you for a future hardship? What unassuming experiences equipped you?

PART 3

Where You
Want to Go

eleven

Acceptance Speech

Please allow me to share an exact recipe for how to put yourself in an extremely uncomfortable environment that plays into your worst insecurities. First, you're going to want to have two work retreats for two different companies overlap and fall on the same week: one in Maui, the other in Mexico. You'll need to have false confidence that you can absolutely do both, in fact you'll WANT to do both. You'll need to travel out of the forty-eight states and experience a five-hour time change after waiting in long airport lines with your four children. And you'll need at least four days and five nights of pushing everyone to their limits in a hotel. This will ensure maximum emotional responses to literally everything! Then after those five days, you'll simply want to leave Maui and fly to Mexico to meet people you've only met online.*

You're going to want to land in Mexico hungry or tired and begin having conversations with groups of people that you do or don't know and make sure to do awkward facial expressions/gratuitous

---

* I'll admit this does sound like a 20/20 murder mystery episode I watch before bed so I can have anxiety in my sleep.

dance moves/baby giraffe gestures. If you've done the above, you may move to the next steps with confidence!

Make sure that you second-guess all your outfit choices (pro tip: consistently be over- or underdressed, wearing bright colors so people have no trouble finding the neon sign that spells A-W-K-W-A-R-D), wonder if you look terrible in a swimsuit, and then get a sunburn on your part to show how incredible your new dandruff snow is. Be sure to have many food intolerances so when it's your turn to order in a group, people wonder if you simply should try some grass clippings from the nearby lawn. Then break out your eighth-grade Spanglish at its finest: "*Sin pan. Sin tomates. Puedo tener* sweet potatoes instead of *blancas*? No? Okay! I'll have the *lechuga* . . . again!"

Once you've done that, you're set for an impending identity crisis. And who hasn't had an identity crisis, especially one that leaves you desperately looking for acceptance even if only from the iguana lounging on your balcony railing?

Yes, that was me. Was it my fault that I had to fly from Hawaii and one work trip on a red-eye to Cabo for another work trip?* What are the chances they would both fall on the same week? And what are the chances that I would have FOMO if I didn't go to both? One hundred percent. I went from fitting in in one place to feeling like I was in sixth grade again, wondering where I'd fit at my new school and if people would like my new, swishy Umbros. My normal habit when in this predicament is to simply withdraw into hermitude, which I like doing to recharge. But it wasn't working because I had a roommate in Mexico. A roommate I didn't want. Not that I didn't want her specifically; I just wanted my own room because I wake up in the middle of the night and sometimes can't go back to sleep. And I am sort of messy and unorganized. And I have four facial tinctures, forty-seven supplements to ensure no autoimmune flare-up, a sound machine, a diffuser with essential oils to help me sleep,

---

* I'm using "work" loosely here, but nonetheless.

a special pillow, and a water bottle that cleans the water because I'm always the one who gets a random, exotic parasite as a souvenir (get behind me, Satan!). Do I use the beer cans from the fridge to reduce eye bags in the morning? YES I DO! It's a lot.

I'm a lot, I say to myself. A room is where you go to just be yourself. And how could I do that and let someone else see all this weirdness?

Weeks before the Mexico trip, the email had gone out for everyone to pick a roommate. I didn't. I emailed the trip coordinator to say I would like to have my own room and I would even do it at my expense. And she responded back that the point of this trip was to connect with people! So rude. If you can even believe that?! *Fine,* I relented. A week later I got an email from a gal going on the trip whom I do adore, and she asked me to be her roomie. "Sure! I would love it!" I replied. *Actually, I would very much NOT love it.**

I arrived exhausted and jet-lagged and with the impending doom of not having my own space. As soon as I got to the lobby, I saw my roommate and she informed me that our room was not ready yet. *Of course! I love sitting in sweats in the heat while jet-lagged and reeking of satanic BO and looking crusty.***

We finally got to our room and Simi, my roommate, was upbeat and kind. We unpacked and made conversation. *Well, she is sort of darling.* I found myself softening. She laughed easily, and we got our suits on. I made sure she knew she could use any of my things. I don't know why I said that, it just came out. "Use this serum. I brought my red light wand; you have to try it. Borrow this, take that, tell me if you need a probiotic." I don't know how to explain it except, "I have a lot of sisters. And I'm just used to sharing."

I figured out by the next day why I had made the sister comment; she *actually* looks like my little sister. They have the same lips and the same high cheekbones, and Simi talks just like my sister. And she has no problem with me being an awkward giraffe. In fact, she

---

* Fake it out alive.
** #goodatfirstimpressions

just kept laughing and teasing me when I stood in my underwear poking my head out from the bathroom, hiding my body, asking the housekeeper for a washcloth using the wrong word.

"*Necessito un* little towel." I drew a small square with my hands and came out of the bathroom, forgetting that I was not dressed, lost in the moment. "*Picento? Picante? Piqueñooooo!*" We cackled as I realized I was definitely underdressed for this interaction.

I kept thinking Simi would do her own thing throughout the day, but she didn't really leave my side. "Simi, I think I've figured it out. You're like my baby sister except you haven't been in rehab and you're a pastor." I didn't mean for it to be so abrupt. She looked up from folding something with big eyes. "I am going to receive that as a compliment." And we burst into laughter. "I wondered what that white powder stuff was in the Ziploc bag!"* There is nothing like the acceptance of a sister. My identity crises started to ease.

The next day by the pool, I met a newish friend, Robin. As she started talking, she said the most hilarious and irreverent things and I began to think I might become her once I hit fifty-eight. And I can't quite pinpoint what it was about her, but I looked at her and she smiled and I felt emotional. *It's my childhood neighbor Caroline Kozar in the flesh. Of course it's not, because Caroline died of breast cancer a decade ago. The last time I saw her was when the cancer had returned and it was bad, but she was still up and around.* When we had finished our visit with Caroline, she stood at the end of the driveway with her hand over her heart, long hair blowing in the breeze, and smiled. I looked through the back windshield until she disappeared, and I promised to sear the memory in my head right then and there.

How bizarre that someone with the same sense of humor, Southern accent, smile lines, eyes, and teeth was in the pool chair next to me, holding a gin and tonic and most of my dearest childhood

---

* It's magnesium, I promise. I have the bowels of a stubborn toddler who has eaten a block of cheese whilst traveling.

memories, which included acceptance of the awkward child next door. I wanted to explain it—how Caroline always invited me in as an unruly and quirky child—but the emotions were in my throat, so I let it go.

The rest of the trip, though, I carried on feeling mostly like I didn't fit in perfectly with any group while receiving acceptance from a few. I tried to be okay with it. I knew who I would have a harder time connecting with because I'd worked with everyone virtually for a year or so, but I have this thing in me that decides I will eventually get them to laugh and, in turn, like me. I'm sure I need to go to therapy for this tactic, but I believe everyone's hard shell can be broken with a self-deprecating story about how I got severely sick on a cruise once—using thespian-like hand movements and silverware from the table and complete with descriptions about an awful bodily function no one should be discussing at dinner. It's bottom-of-the-barrel humor, but no one gets trophies based on exactly how they make people laugh. Here is your servant, O God.

Not everyone gets my humor, or my personality, for that matter. But I really, really want them to. To know me is to know I love all things Enneagram, that personality/character trait assessment from the '70s that's enjoying new popularity lately. Some people like to use it to validate themselves and not feel alone (that's awesome!), and some people like to use it to understand other people, as it is a magical cheat sheet. The answers are, in fact, in the back of the book! For someone who absolutely cheated her way through algebra because her brain doesn't understand number-y things, this is a true blessing. I am an Enneagram Seven: I like a lot of fun and stimulation, have extreme fear of missing out, love traveling and adventures even though they make me so uncomfortable, have one million friends including the mailman and all dogs, and I am annoyingly enthusiastic about ANYTHING I am interested in and will make sure to tell you about it. But say you're a Four—dark and moody in the best way, pensive, always in your thoughts, need little stimulation, eager to be unique and mysterious, and good with having just a few close friends—then a Seven comes along and asks you if you want to go skinny-dipping in a foreign country with the thirty-eight ducks you just caught while taking Jell-O shots.* That may or may not have been my gallant approach in Mexico.

I specifically sought out those whom I hadn't had a chance to connect with. You know, the ones who were likely the Enneagram number (or the personality as a whole) I have a hard time understanding. They stare wide-eyed as I tell a joke and only laugh because they can see it's supposed to be funny, but they really don't get it. If you have to say the punch line twice, just know you've failed and should slink into a nearby cactus for comfort. By the end of the trip, I'd had great conversations with most everyone, great softenings, and more compassion, but I still felt like I did *not* belong. Even on the last morning, I skipped around at breakfast making sure I said hello and goodbye, even inserting myself a wee bit awkwardly into various breakfast groups. Then I stole a quiet, last walk alone, and I eye-rolled at myself. The lingering non-fitting-in-ness was relentless and gnawing. We were in a beautiful location with palm trees and good people working to write and say good things about God, all of us so different. Yet internally, ugly insecurity still ruled, although it really had nothing to do with them.

By the time I got to the airport to go home, I was exhausted and feeling a lot. I had told my husband some of the feelings, and he had said what he always says: "It's probably your inner dialogue that's not telling you the truth." *Wise words, I guess. But I'd rather think that everyone hates me, sir! That's easier than confronting identity issues with God.*

I got to check in at the airport with a gal from our trip named Jenn who was on my flight out. She mothered me through each process of international travel, like wrangling a baby giraffe with luggage. We knew our seats weren't together, so once we got to the plane, we split.

---

* I have only done one of those things, so I'll let you guess.

When I got to my row, my seat was in between two men. The one on the aisle smiled big and asked, "Are you dead set on this middle seat? Or would you like the window seat up front? My wife is up there, and I think she'd trade you." I looked over to see the woman was sitting by Jenn. I beamed. "Of course!" It would be coincidental, except I know that God's character is not happenstance—it's very much on purpose.

I truly need a handler when I travel, and won't the Lord provide it? Lucky her! Jenn reminded me of my angel assistant at home who is helping me organize and downsize, ever so gently moving me away from my hoarder tendencies. I immediately felt comforted sitting next to Jenn. I thanked God for the little breadcrumbs of acceptance I had found on this trip with Simi and with Robin and now with Jenn. On the way to our connecting flight, we had lots of good conversations and some decompression. We are both Sevens, and we laughed about our personalities together. It was nice to feel known and accepted again.*

At one point in our long flight, she shared a story from Mexico. Someone asked the people in a particular group that Jenn randomly happened to be in (*the* particular group of people I kept thinking was so annoyed with me), "What is the Enneagram you have the most trouble with?" The resounding response? "SEVENS!"

She said that it was so funny to admit she was a Seven, but they had a great conversation about their differences. For a minute, I stopped listening. *Of course they don't like me. It was not all in my head. I must have been so annoying, trying so hard to connect with them. And here I thought we made some progress! How foolish . . . see, YOU ARE too much.*

I pretended to carry on, but inside my feelings were hurt. So I focused on editing photos from the trips to take my mind off the

---

* These interactions can affirm who we are and who we are meant to be, but whether we feel accepted or not, we still have to be who God made us to be.

whole painful situation. As I looked through the photos, I stopped at one of the white planks on the sand made for wheelchair access to the cabanas. It looked like an exact cross. Then it struck me: this was between me and God.

Wasn't he using this event at my weakest to show me where my identity lay? I had been writing and speaking on how to operate in your God-given you-ness, and yet here I was struggling with mine. It doesn't matter how much personal development I do, how much I mature and age, how much I think I'm relying on Christ. On this side of heaven, I will continually have opportunities to find my way back to him. I will desperately need to find my identity in Christ over and over.

I don't believe I am a failure for needing Jesus like this. This is why he came. This is where the cross meets me: smack-dab in the middle of my deepest insecurities. I settled my heart and prayed that God would remind me who I was. *I made you annoyingly enthusiastic. I made you just so, with just this much energy, with this much eagerness to seek out those who reject you with a dance move and a joke.* This isn't about others; they didn't make me feel this way. And it isn't necessarily about a false dialogue or even about my greatest fears being realized: *What if you are, in fact, too much for them? Or what if you're making it all up?* Whether I'm accepted or rejected by humans, he remains the same. His acceptance of me remains the same. The good news, and the only news that will satisfy me in my bones, is that I am too much; my much-ness speaks to his abundance, his creativity, his humor, his seriousness, his mind, his uniqueness, his well-roundedness.

Why is seriousness seen as more spiritual than hilariousness when they both reflect him? Or who is to say the one who plays music is better than the person who creates with paint? Is the written word more important than the spoken word? Is a doctor more important than a Sunday school teacher? Is a mother who works outside the home more valuable than a mother who does not? Or what if she never becomes a mother? Is the eye more important than the hand?

We know the answer. (See 1 Corinthians 12.) Yet we tend to want to find our identity and approval in humans more than we wish we did. But we can't ride on the acceptance of others, nor get derailed by their rejection.

I remember when my sister was having a particularly difficult day, feeling like a bad mom. I told her about the time I was potty training my oldest son, who was then three. When we were outside, I told him if it was an emergency and he couldn't hold it, he could simply "pee on a tree" (please remember I am from Texas). Upon hearing my infant daughter crying inside, I went in to change her and get ready to nurse. As I settled on the couch, I watched my toddler from the huge front window digging in the dirt. In a matter of moments, he became frantic, pulled his pants down, squatted, and pooped on the driveway! I couldn't get up fast enough to make him stop, so by the time I got out there it was too late. I wondered what people driving by were thinking. *Who lets their child poop on the driveway?*

As my sister and I laughed about this story, she said something I haven't forgotten: "I am so thankful my identity is not in being a good mother. Because I'm failing."

When you're knee-deep in an intense time, like mothering lots of little humans or managing unruly employees, it can be tempting to base your identity on those roles. But as my sister said, we're failing, and we miss the mark. And when we fail, because we will, we must have something greater than our titles or idols, which will never satisfy.

Looking at everything eternally flips the coin. My roles become avenues to explore who God made me to be. My failures point me to take on his identity and let go of mine; those failures serve as arrows to show me a new direction, always for my good.

If we believe that all personalities and giftings and skills and talents point us to our need to be enveloped in the most important identity, which is *covered* in Christ, if we *could* believe that, if God could help our unbelief, wouldn't it be the most unifying concept on the planet among believers? Wouldn't it free us all to run with wild abandon, permission slips in hand, setting the world on fire with our unique imprints because they are his unique imprints? A flashlight showing the way to the cross, where we are all important to God's global family?

We need to know deep in our hearts that he has invited us into a great mission! "You're kingdom subjects. Now live like it. Live out your God-created identity" (Matthew 5:48 MSG).

> *Look for the host. Do you see him across the room, making his way toward you, beaming? You belong here.*

Remember, there's a place for you at the table where you don't have to elbow others, beat them to the best seat, scrounge for scraps, or sneak in the back door and take someone else's spot. No, look for the host. Do you see him across the room, making his way toward you, beaming? You belong here. You are wanted here. You have a seat. Your plate is full of satisfying, gorgeous foods, not just grass clippings. And your cup is overflowing. That is how we live sufficiently full in an empty world of unsatisfying identities that aren't ours to take on. It's the most unifying, permisionslippyest, freedom-inducing news!

Following Your Breadcrumbs

We can find a million reasons to refrain from being who we really are. Usually, they come from messages we've heard from parents, friends, mean girls, the media, or even church leaders. As we grow up, we notice what makes us "acceptable" or "accepted" and adjust our behavior to fit into that ecosystem. Lately, I've been asking myself, What is the script I'm rehearsing consistently in my head? *Scripts sound a lot like insecurities, so if you can find those, you usually can find a script such as* "I can't do this. I am a fake!" *Eventually, we all start believing what we rehearse.*

My treasure map word:
LEARNER, EXPANDER, WRITER

Is there a place in your life where you believe you're too much or not enough? Maybe people have straight up said it to you and you took it as truth.

What are those personality traits you tend to hold back so others accept you? Are there ways you've changed to fit in? Where does the cross intersect these insecurities?

Bonus: I often find myself not being able to say no to travel opportunities. It awakens something inside of me and compels me to grow in places I wouldn't normally if I stayed at home. I am most uncomfortable when I travel, but I also tend to grow the most! Is there an activity in your life that you can't seem to say no to, that you even look forward to, but it remains uncomfortable at times?

twelve

The MiraculASS
Transformation

took a public speaking class in college. I tell myself I did it because it was required to graduate. God let me hang on to that delusion for quite some time. Believe me, I was not an overachiever who took classes "just for fun."

Our elderly teacher wore a toupee, had the deep voice of a chain smoker (I saw him once on a smoke break *gasp*), and was rather funny. He had obviously given these lectures over and over because they rolled off his tongue, practiced and eloquent with well-timed zingers. I decided I would probably be okay at this class because of him, except for the small fact that I hated public speaking. My thoughts are jumbled—*why are the campus squirrels overweight? Should I tell my roommates I'm the one feeding the stray cat? How many times can you skip this particular class and still pass?*—and I have a lot of them all at once. This guy was telling me I needed to organize those thoughts and mostly memorize a whole speech, clearly and succinctly, WITHOUT telling people I was about to poop my pants. Rule Number One from Mr. Grigsby: "You mustn't tell people how nervous you are. We already know how damn nervous you are. You're all sweating like a Chick-fil-A cow lost at the Golden Corral." *Got it—don't tell everyone what they already know.* Rule Number Two: Don't take a number two in front of your peers.

For the final, we had to give a speech using the accumulation of skills we had learned that semester covering a topic of our choice, as long as we were passionate about it. After each speech, the rest of the class would fill out a short but damning evaluation on what they liked and how the speaker could improve. *If they could find anything.* I thought long and hard for over three minutes and decided to speak on how to get saved, in case everyone in that class died of an overly religious college student boring them to death. I already had a pamphlet in my backpack from a Christian campus meeting that laid out the steps to salvation, so it basically did the work for me. And while I loved God dearly, sometimes obnoxiously, I loved half-assing my assignments even more.

On the morning of my speech, I decided to wear an above-the-knee, denim, spaghetti-strap dress with a tank underneath and platform sandals. This was to signal that I was wholesome but also was up for a good make-out sesh. *See my kneecaps?!* Did they know I had a cross with a Jesus Fish tattoo on my hip bone underneath that dress? Nope! How scandalous.* Three people went ahead of me. So like a good peer, I rehearsed my three-minute speech ad nauseam while ignoring theirs.

I don't remember anything about my speech except that I was sweating pretty hard, as Mr. Grigsby said I would, and I mistakenly said, "Romans Row" (Jami version?). Come to find out from one of the peer evaluations, it was "Romans Road." *My bad, but the spirit can still work through my errors, Brody.* Romans Row-Road goes something like this: We are all sinners, the price for sin is hell (a real heartwarming tale; *Chicken Soup for the Wayward Collegiate Soul*, author: Satan), we need a Savior, and if you ask him to save you, he will. Lastly, First Book

* Insert music: "My knees, my caps . . . my denim, and my tatts."

of Opinions, if you squeeze the note card hard enough, it will practically stop shaking and lock your thumb up for a good hour afterward.

I finished and was neither displeased nor pleased. All I could feel was that my bowels were calling, and I would need to exit this classroom stat! As he did with all students, Mr. Grigsby summed up my speech while I took my seat. "Okay, Ms. Baker, thank you for taking us to church several days early, this fine Friday. Basically, you're saying if you're a good person, you'll go to heaven. Round of applause for Ms. Baker. Brody, you're next."

How had my teacher gotten the exact opposite point of my speech? *No, we are sinners! We're the worst. He still loves us. WELP, I guess Mr. Grigsby isn't getting into the pearly gates because of me!* Were my kneecaps too distracting, or was I just bad at public speaking? It must have been the latter because I made sure to shave and lotion that morning, and my kneecaps were *shining* as unto the Lord. While I passed the class with a B (for Bad at sharing the gospel), I decided neither public speaking nor Algebra 2 (which I had to take thrice) would be my strong suits in life.

But as life would have it, I was regularly put in front of some kind of a pulpit, mostly to share our marriage story of forgiveness. While I wasn't a polished speaker, I was confident the message of redemption would strongly make up for all the poor college students I had led astray with an unclear speech assignment of old. I started with Mothers of Preschoolers (MOPS*) because they were desperate and willing to listen to anything if there was a modicum of silence and their kids weren't crawling on them. A win-win. MOPS groups paid me in sponge-painted dish towels and strange Baptist church cookbooks (with the Crock-Pot wieners in the jelly). But I was determined to keep sharing what God had done, perhaps even as obnoxiously as denim-dress-college-Jami. It felt like the message was bigger than the skill—and who cared anyway? *I wasn't ever going to be on a main stage anywhere.*

* what is a more flattering title for mothers?!

151

Except I knew in the back of my mind that was not true. Early on in my separation from my husband after discovering the affair, I was having weird dreams. Except I wasn't quite asleep (this is where you can stop reading if I'm getting too woo-woo for you). In one of those dreams, I was on a big stage where I was the speaker and my husband—who, at the time, I was sure I was divorcing—was introducing me. I turned around to see a very large crowd and knew I was supposed to tell this message to whoever would listen. In my more awake hours, getting on a big stage was not even a desire. In fact, I would rather not poop my pants or sweat profusely and nervously in public. I just wanted to heal. I didn't know if I was going to even have a marriage, let alone become a public speaker! The crevasse from point A to point B was too large to cross for both of those things and was filled with a moat of giant alligators and crustaceans and furry peaches, not to mention lots of difficult tasks I didn't feel equipped to do.

But eventually I crossed the moat on one front: our marriage began to heal. It was enough for me for a long time and all I had energy for. But something strange also kept happening: I kept saying yes to speaking events, including larger church retreats when I could, and sometimes I would even get real money!* I had no business being up on a stage, no credentials, not the best at it, no one raving about my talent in communication. Just a broken marriage that God healed and God picking someone weak. "Ah yes, I will take the most inept person here . . ." [Looks around the crowd to find me avoiding eye contact.] "Yes, you, lady crying and holding the lingerie at the overwhelmingly fragrant Victoria's Secret while telling the eighteen-year-old cashier she MUST take this back because you're getting a divorce . . . winner, winner!"

Pulling out his cloud clipboard, he continues, "Sweats profusely getting in front of people, CHECK. Has a possible leaky gut and will possibly nervous poop before each speaking event, CHECK.

* Let me repeat: I did NOT want to speak in front of anybody!

Deathly afraid of crustaceans and hates peaches, which are in her imaginary moat, CHECK." I didn't love it; I would rather have been writing or washing my hair. (That's a lie. I'm on day forty-five of dry shampoo.) But I was being obedient to the call, and I couldn't help it. God must have a sense of humor if he picked me to do this kind of work.

It was exactly this kind of work that brought me to the main stage at an essential oils (EO) conference. I saw you laugh. *A conference all about essential oils? How absurd!* But before you poo-poo it, you need to settle down and know that I beat you to it. I made fun of my best friend for going the year before. Then I was there the next year because eating my words is delicious. At my first EO conference, I saw a lady with a cat in a stroller and people wearing lanyards with flair (WITH FLAIR!), and it smelled like Care Bear halitosis. So it's pretty magical, one could say.* At that first conference, I sat high in the bleachers and looked down to where all the people who were at the top of the company sat. Something in my heart said, "I'll get there one day." Which is odd for me because I am not really the achieving-rank type (see also my inability to finish anything, including college, or come take a peek at my sock pile).

The next year, I worked hard and made a higher rank and snuck down to the bottom floor with my mom and sister, pretending to be one of the "diamonds" so I could watch Lady A perform a concert.** The year after that, I was one of the high rankers and watched the event from the ground floor. FYI: listening to the keynote from down there sounds the same as in the rafters, but it didn't stop me from being proud of my hard work. While I listened to the speaker

---

* Since then, I've been to many of these conferences. It's the biggest sales training event and I get to see my team and my friends—and everyone smells really, really, like outrageously good.

** Faking your way through it sometimes works, or maybe it was just belief that the stirring inside me wasn't from me anyway.

153

from up close, something inside me said, "I'm going to be up there one day." Except being onstage sounded abysmal. *No, thank you.*

Several months passed, and I opened an email to find a request for me to speak. I had spoken at a breakout session before, maybe to one hundred people, and enjoyed it. I was assuming they wanted me to do this again, so without reading any of the details (very common of my beautiful personality), I accepted. I had months to think about my topic. Instead, I waited until the last minute when they said I had to rehearse my talk in front of the compliance department. *How odd, this must be new. They didn't make me do that last year.* I scoured the email for details on what was required and noticed something: "All our main-stage speakers are required to . . ." My eyes got huge and my stomach tightened. Read it again. M-a-i-n-s-t-a-g-e! More like m-a-y-d-a-y! *Why am I like this?!* I am sure this is when God came out from the clouds with his clipboard and flowy hair and was like, "LOL. See, I knew you wouldn't accept if you read the details, so I distracted you with a dog. Or was it a squirrel? Get it!" It was too close to the event to back out.

I decided I would revamp the talk I had given to my own team at a retreat about connecting to and rediscovering themselves, something I was passionate about and still am today. Everything difficult that has brought them here, everything that they love today, everything that they dream about . . . it's on purpose. It was the only message I cared to speak about, and like before, my passion would have to carry me through this because Lord knows I was not polished enough to speak to forty thousand people.

To boot, they also told me I would have to make a PowerPoint. Listen, I am skilled at a few things, but one of them is not Power-Point. So I decided to go rogue and make a PowerPoint so bad that it would be good. I asked my mother to find a picture of me as a kid selling rocks.

"Why in the world would I have a picture of you selling rocks?"

"Because people take pictures of their kids selling Girl Scout Cookies," I retorted.

"Well, that's because that's cute," she said, laughing.

If I couldn't find a picture of me selling rocks, I would simply have to superimpose my adult head on a picture of a kid with a wagon and add fake rocks in the wagon. It looked terrib . . . ly good. *If it's funny to me, maybe it will be funny to them.* I continued the slides, one after the other, wondering if the compliance team would let me show them or make me redo them. Someone must have been sick that day because they accepted the slides. I practiced the talk three times and wrote it out. I prayed that God would help me because I never stay on script. *Just make it meaningful. Let them get past me.*

My goal was to make it entertaining and to show them that I was obviously not the most qualified, but I did have something I couldn't help but tell them about. My intro would start with everyone dancing, my PowerPoint would be hilariously terrible, and in the end, it would be all about them. I wouldn't let them leave without knowing that all the good, terrible, natural gifts, learned skills, old jobs, and people who have influenced them for better or worse will all be used for their good if they chose to see it that way. Maybe we would laugh and cry our way through it, but I would show them how my husband cheating on me actually got me all the way to that stage even though they appeared to have nothing in common.

I stood backstage so nervous. I had to go to the bathroom for *various* reasons, but also to stuff paper towels in my armpits. I decided I would pull out the makeshift armpit pads right before I went on stage.* As I heard someone introduce me, I thought maybe I'd just run away. *No, you have to have this baby!* My intro music started (compliance had denied it, but I had asked the backstage guys to play it anyway, and they agreed). *Okay, God, do the work.* I forgot that the paper towels were in and walked out to cheers and an eruption of laughter. "Well, at least this is on brand. Guys, you'd

---

* As I am writing this, my heart rate is a calm and collected nineteen thousand beats per minute, and I am practicing belly breaths that I learned from my daughter Penelope, age ten.

be sweating too if you had to get up here. Is there an oil for this?" More laughing. Something was happening in my heart. *Am I . . . liking this?*

I did my intro, and as I got into making sense of the terrible circumstances that have happened, I told them about our marriage being redeemed. In the corporate world, you aren't able to talk about God, but I told them a story about a guy whose brothers were terrible to him, beat him up, and sold him into slavery. How he spent time in jail falsely accused, but how in the end, he was royalty. He could have been bitter, but he remained soft. He believed it would have a purpose. The last line of the famous story goes something like this: "What you meant for evil for me, God meant for good."* Lightbulbs were going off, and I could feel the electricity.

Public speaking finally felt good even though the slides were not formatted for the screen. I could tell all the way through, but they were already so awful, no one noticed—until the final slide that was supposed to say "Your life is a freaking treasure" looked like this:

You're Life
Is a
Freakin
G
Treasure

I looked up at the screen and looked back at the audience and said, "Man, I'm good at this!" Then I sang, "You're life is a freeeeeakin G treasurrrre," to the tune of the famous rap song "Nuthin' but a 'G' Thang" by Dr. Dre. The crowd was laughing and engaged and I felt like a magician pulling rabbits out of a hat . . . errr . . . Power-Point. Some kind of magic was happening in my heart, some kind of transformation. Like I was turning into a butterfly—or maybe less eloquently, like when God made the ass speak, which is still a

---

* See Genesis 50:20.

pretty cool miracle even if it's not parting the Red Sea or anything. God already parted the Red Sea in my marriage, so I was willing to become the ass who spoke.

At the end, the crowd cheered, not because I was polished, but because I was up there being myself and telling them to do the same. I was light and free because I obviously (quite obviously) really believed the message I was speaking.

The gospel sometimes doesn't look like someone in a denim dress stating Romans Road to a forced audience. It sometimes looks like being on the Road with them, shining light on hidden rocks, mudholes, awful crustaceans, furry peaches, and thrashing alligators in the moat below. Yes, they are real, but so is this flashlight and so is this bridge over the moat.

· · · · · · · · · · **Following Your Breadcrumbs** · · · · · · · · · ·

God continues to put some things in front of us that we feel ill-equipped to do. Why does this keep happening?! Over and over? At some point, acknowledging a pattern in your life might help you to embrace it instead of deny it. It's like writing this book. I was sometimes frustrated that people kept asking me to write about this or that. I am not consistent; I am not particularly good at grammar or spelling or taming the squirrels in my thoughts (just ask my editors!). But I kept finding myself in the position to write. People kept asking me to write for this magazine or that blog. In fact, one of my editors for this book emailed me once a year asking me to write a book. I mostly ignored him, until I didn't, and here we are! It wasn't that I felt I was gifted at writing. In fact, it was the opposite; but the opportunities kept showing up.

My treasure map word:
PUBLIC SPEAKER

What's an area where you don't feel equipped, but it keeps showing up?

Often we don't get to see the big picture while we're in the process of learning, but where might God be leading you with a skill you're practicing? Can you see where it is producing fruit?

Is there an affection for something that God has grown in you over time and now you see his hand in it?

What do you catch yourself saying that you're going to do some day, but then you blow it off or make a joke of it? Or what do you have a desire to do but think is too preposterous or ridiculous?

thirteen

Dream On

I am pretty good at daydreaming. I've had forty years to practice, and I'm married to a non-daydreamer. I thought everyone lived up in the clouds like me until I married Nato and he consistently asked me, "What are you thinking about?" when my eyes glazed over. I guess daydreaming has a look. But more important, he doesn't naturally daydream, so I have to keep people like him in mind. Daydreaming may be easy for me, but it's okay if it's not for you! I am not naturally good at numbers or mail or being on time, and that's why I found Nan in Dallas, who whips me into financial shape every month and continually asks what Cargo Largo is on my receipts.* Essentially, I need people who are gifted in areas I'm not so I don't land in jail for bad accounting. That's why my breadcrumbs are for me and yours are just for you. Mine are gluten-free anyway. Luckily, you won't go to jail for not daydreaming, but think of me as your bail bonds lady for your brain.

....

* It's a discount store I love, but I tell her it's a doctor's office I visit for an ongoing issue with my pet salamander.

I even take daydreaming on the road. I remember a time I was teaching my team to daydream at a retreat in 2018. "Imagine yourself smiling ear to ear. . . . Where are you in your mind? Who is with you? And what are you doing?"

When I answered these questions for the first time myself, I saw water. The light was reflecting off it. I was with my family, and I was lying in the sun while they splashed around. Their laughter echoed in the back of my mind. I didn't know where I was, but it felt idyllic. Unfortunately for that dream, I am not a water person at all! I get carsick on winding lake roads even when I'm driving. I am concerned about what's under the water and whether it will destroy my glued-on eyelashes or if I will be the one who gets the flesh-eating parasite I saw on the Discovery Channel by simply dipping my toes in. I didn't grow up around any water in the landlocked Texas Panhandle. I didn't know if the water in my daydream was a lake or a river or an ocean, although I can tell you it definitely wasn't a horse trough. *Why was I dreaming of water?* I tucked it away. *Just another daydream, and I'll likely have four hundred more by the time I go to bed.*

Six months later, we found ourselves in possession of a large lake house that needed lots of work. Lots of renovations, lots of vision, and, well, lots of swimming in the lake with the kids. As you know, I was resistant to the lake-lady vibe. My husband would always choose lake vacations, and I found them unappealing and stressful. I can remember telling him to give up on his dream of ever having a lake house or marry someone different.* How encouraging and sweet was I in my younger years? But I am telling you, the pull of the water! The pull of that house. The project. The daydreaming of the water. My husband's dream to have a lake house. It all led to that lake property we weren't even looking for. His breadcrumbs

* Pro tip: It's not cool to squash other people's breadcrumbs just because they're not like yours. We need the ryes and the sourdoughs just as much as we need the ciabattas.

were converging with mine, helping me see clearly that we were on the right path together. And while I had no clue what I was doing, I couldn't help but be pulled right to that spot. It was almost like all our previous investments, all our previous renovation knowledge, all our failed dreams, all our daydreams were the breadcrumbs that led us there, right where we were supposed to be, although I wouldn't have knowingly chosen it on my own.

Several years later at a larger event, I revisited the daydreaming concept. I asked the crowd to close their eyes and visualize smiling ear to ear. *Where are you, who are you with, and what are you doing?* Because apparently, I am entranced by this question and can't let a good moment of silence pass without filling it with my own daydreams.

I did the activity with the audience. In a flash, I was in the coffee shop we had bought. My husband and the kids and I were all working on odds and ends, getting it ready to open. I was beaming. I didn't see water this time, albeit we were still close to the lake, but we were making a business.

A daydream can often change as fast as you do, or it may stay with you a long time. Some daydreams don't come to fruition. But that doesn't make the act of dreaming any less valuable or worthwhile. I was giving myself space for an opportunity to envision my heart's desires: I *love* making new businesses and streams of income. That brings me joy—I think on it, scheme on it, daydream about it. So while you may think daydreaming might be reserved for those creatives or the ones who can't stay focused, dreaming is for everyone because it is an act of God. He dreamed up the world. He dreamed up a seal (did he laugh when he added whiskers?), and he dreamed up you and me. He created us in his image. It is in our nature to reflect him, so you have permission to dream on. Practice it; you'll get better and better with more and more details. And why not right now?

> *Some daydreams don't come to fruition. But that doesn't make the act of dreaming any less valuable or worthwhile.*

As you know by now, the questions come at the end of the chapter. But I can't do that here. The world needs your own unique dream, with your own unique spin and your unique talents. Perhaps you're like my husband . . . he genuinely wants to help, and maybe you do too. It's easier and more natural for him to walk alongside others and make their dreams become reality. He will make my dream his because, apparently, he's more of an unselfish angel than I am. But I'm asking you to put on your oxygen mask first. That will come as second nature to some women (maybe you're like me and you could do it in your sleep—see what I did there?). For others, the dreaming might feel wonky. Either way, the dream needs to be purely yours. So here's what I want you to do.

Close your eyes.

I take that back, read the next few lines first, then close your eyes.

You're smiling ear to ear. (Really. You have to smile hard.)

Where are you in your mind?

Now look further. Who is with you?

And even further—what are you doing?

If it doesn't come right away, sit in silence for a bit and ask the questions again.*

Congratulations, you just daydreamed! Write down what you pictured immediately, and we'll expand on it later.

God is a God of details—and he's in those daydream details—but he is also mysterious. Here's the thing about daydreams: like breadcrumbs, they only show you part of the way, not the whole journey. God gives a glimpse so you know which direction to go, and then you start moving. That's the beauty of it—breadcrumbs force you to rely on God. They bring you back to him because he is the one leaving the breadcrumbs. If we had the whole picture and knew all the answers, all the twists, all the turns, then we wouldn't have to

* I'm peeking with one eye to see if you're really closing your eyes and smiling.

164

rely on him or come back to him or find him. We would strike out on our own, thinking we had all the answers. He gives us a part, just the next few steps or just the next picture or just the next dream. We have to trust him and trust that following the breadcrumbs, being who we are meant to be and doing what we are meant to do, is the only way to stay on our path.

Speaking of trusting God, we surprisingly sold the giant lake house and are renting a small 800-square-foot cottage until we figure out what we want to do next. The market isn't ripe for buying, and building costs are astronomical. We are just sitting ducks (pun intended). What is God doing? What is next? We truly have no clue. I have ideas to scale the coffee shop and ideas for a new restaurant concept, but the restaurateur I pitched it to hasn't gotten back to me, and my husband has reminded me that most restaurants fail. I can't help but think of the time I told him to give up on his lake dream and how I was wrong, so I'm still holding out hope. I can't tie this up in a bow and tell you how everything is going to pan out. But can I tell you what I'm doing now? I'm taking my own advice.

In essence, I'm praying for manna from heaven, for God to provide the sustenance of wisdom. I'm looking for crumbs and even finding some. I'm confident I'll keep finding them. It's unsettling to be on what feels like a dark path at times, but I know how this goes. Sometimes you lean on old faith to get you moving forward. I remember what God has done in the past. I remember that I'm still the eight-year-old kid selling rocks. I remember that when things feel confusing, devastating, or even joyful and fun that God doesn't change and has been with me the whole way making all things work for my good. He says, "Do not fear," and do you know what accompanies that command? He says, "For I am with you."* He promises that in fear, in those shaking steps forward, he will give us his presence.

---

* "Fear not, for I am with you; be not dismayed, for I am your God; I will strengthen you, I will help you, I will uphold you with my righteous right hand" (Isaiah 41:10).

Sometimes we have to take a break on the journey and wait. Sit down for a breather. Hang out until God drops the next crumb. There is no shame in looking around and not really seeing anything up ahead, trusting that God will provide for you even in the waiting. He is there in the wilderness too.

In thinking forward, on my own path, I don't have all the answers as to which direction to go. I was just sitting on the couch talking with my husband about this last night. We came to the conclusion that we'll have to believe that the same God who gave us direction along the way in the past is able to do it again. It's a fork in the road. I can practice hope, or I can practice despair. And I'll tell you what I did when my husband left for his evening meeting. I closed my eyes and asked myself, "Where are you? Who are you with? What are you doing?" It was quiet except for Greta, my Boston terrier, boorishly snoring.

God, you'll have to give me a dream. I don't see anything. I had a low-key headache that was trying to distract me. I squinted to get past it, to see if there was light somewhere in this tunnel. More silence. But in the distance, there was light. Then there I was all dressed up; I could feel my skirt brushing against my shins. The light streamed in from stage right and I was looking at women in an audience, telling them that their dreams were important and real. I was holding up a permission slip* with excitement, and I was sweating as usual, but this time I had no armpit pads!

When I opened my eyes, I was still smiling.

I may not open a new restaurant (could be God's protection), we may not get to renovate another lake house (we'll love resting a bit), I may fail at scaling the coffee shop (perhaps it doesn't need to scale), this book may flop (still so proud that I finished it!), and I may never get to stand onstage and tell you about it. But the breadcrumbs keep showing me that I'm made to be an entrepreneur, made to be writing, made to be speaking, made to be fixing up spaces, made to

---

* Like you get in the principal's office.

166

be showing up just like this. Even if this is a pipe dream, it's good to practice dreaming. It helps me become more me. Light and free from who I wish I were, who others think I should be, step by step becoming the me-est me God made me to be.*

I become more me by getting my hopes up.

I didn't used to live that way. I used to believe the crowd yelling, "Dreams mostly don't come true! Don't expect joy! A bad thing could happen right around the corner and ruin everything!" I would think I needed to put my head down and just suffer through life like a grumpy cat in the rain with no umbrella. But that isn't how God tells us to pray. He asks us to pray like this: "Your kingdom come . . . on earth as it is in heaven" (Matthew 6:10). He tells us to pray for glimmers of heaven. And heaven is where joy is the most realized, where we will all be the most realized version of ourselves, where we will all be free from the constraints of this world. It's the most perfect of perfect places. And when we dream, we get to look for those slivers of heaven to come to earth. One of those heavenly slivers is doing exactly what you're made to do with no false self, no cynicism, just pure-of-heart hope that God will accomplish something good through you. Today. Tomorrow. Someday.

I become more me by getting my hopes up.

I assure you that dreams do come true because we are God's dreams, and we are here. And so are the sun and the moon and the ocean and all the fish we haven't even discovered (minus flesh-eating parasites, they can all go to hell). While many humans live with the crushing weight of cynicism, believers have the unique opportunity to live as people marked by hope.** He will make your dream come to fruition in some way—and especially in ways you haven't thought of yet. He will provide the path, and the flashlight and the

* T-shirts to follow . . . new merch line?? See, I can't help it.
** Here's where I hold your face in my hands and look you in the eyes: If God put a dream in your heart, it is not dumb.

breadcrumbs and the storms and the cleft and the sunshine. And it will have always been about you believing him. Believing what he says about you and who he called you to be. Don't let me fool you; don't let anyone actually. No one has it figured out. We are all in process, we are all doing it a little afraid, and we are all wondering if we are foolish for following the mystery of God's ways sometimes. Today I am walking you home on your path with my flashlight, and one day I'll need you to do that for me. We'll find our way eventually, one foot in front of the other. Hansel and Gretel all the way to the place we were meant to be: home in him, home in who we were meant to be all along.

· · · · · · · · · · · **Following Your Breadcrumbs** · · · · · · · · · ·

Everyone thinks a dream is supposed to end in some big success. But the act of dreaming itself is an exercise in hope. I remember several life-giving voice messages back and forth with some of my best friends. One friend said, "I have this crazy idea, and I've never said it out loud because it just feels dumb." It was fun to laugh and dream and affirm all of it, even if it may never come to be. It just felt good to be talking ideas, to be dreaming together. In fact, it endeared us to each other, to be talking about our hopes and dreams, because I think it speaks to the eternal attribute of hope. It speaks to the great idea maker himself. I believe God delights in us as we hope, even if it never comes to be. But what's scarier than it not happening is . . . what if it does? Out of the forty-three dreams my friends and I discussed, we can't let go of a single one and still talk about them today. It may turn out to be something. (I guess you'll have to wait to see if our duck 'n' dog farm/spiritual development Airstream comes to fruition! JK, apparently ducks poop a lot so I'm out.)

168

My treasure map word:
VISIONARY

Is there a dream you have that you've decided is dumb or unworthy or that you've pushed aside because it's too unrealistic?

Revisit that dream and write out what is compelling about it.

Where are the breadcrumbs in that daydream?

I hope you also wrote down your daydream from earlier in the chapter. What are the details?

What are the unknowns?

What about the dream makes you smile?

How do you need God to meet you in the unknown of your purpose or future?

fourteen

Now What?

I hope you took the time to reflect on your breadcrumbs at the end of each chapter. In fact, YOU are the most important part of this book. I wrote this book thinking about you scribbling down on your treasure map and seeing lightbulbs go off! If you haven't taken the time to adequately brain dump, please do that first before carrying on to this activity; otherwise it will be like pulling teeth.*

Where do all these breadcrumbs lead? What is the treasure? The treasure is YOU, the you God meant you to be. The treasure is discovering that God was doing everything in your life on purpose. He was and is weaving a grand story through you so that you will see him more clearly. And when you see him more clearly, you see yourself rightly. You see yourself with confidence to be just you. Those breadcrumbs tell you who YOU are and where you're going! And it's pretty exciting!

. . . .

* Flashbacks to being ten and having teeth extracted to make space for the new teeth coming in, and it really is that unpleasant! It's much easier to let them fall out while eating a baguette.

173

On page 179, you'll find a map with fill in the blanks. From each of the "Following Your Breadcrumbs" brain dumps at the end of the chapters, try to pick out one word or a small phrase that best describes your answers. Jot it on the map. There is no right or wrong answer; this is just for you. No one else is going to see this unless you want to show them how weird God made you. I found that a lot of my words ended in -er. Like Teacher, Sower, Dreamer. If you're thinking, *This is too abstract for me*, I get it.

So I'm going to go all high school English teacher on you. In my short stint of crash-course educating, I learned to quickly find themes in chapters and books to help my students understand the whole work. After reading a book, it's good to look back over it and find themes, patterns, and consistencies to help you understand the whole of the work and to see that the author wasn't just telling a good story. He was saying something important. For instance, in *The Great Gatsby*, you can see the author is struggling with the concept of the American Dream: a person gets it all and still feels empty and continually searches for fulfillment (the gospel according to Gatsby, but isn't this just Ecclesiastes?).

This is what we're doing now: we're looking for themes in our own lives. There's no googling the answers or cheating our way through the chapters; we must do the work. And I slightly cringe at writing this for fear of sounding very LIVE-LAUGH-LOVE-ish, but in writing this book, teaching it, and analyzing my own life, I've found that the work is the treasure. The journey of discovering is where you'll find joy.

In each part of your journaling and documenting, you can find themes that continually show up too. If you get nitty-gritty, they present themselves in the form of adjectives, traits, and -ing words. Wow, I think I really am a high school English teacher at the chalkboard pointing and circling! This twelve-dollar sweater vest does give me magical guiding powers. I hope you aren't rolling your eyes and wanting class to be over so you can eat that horrible, soggy, square pizza and the giant, undercooked cookie at lunch that surely gave us all an underlying autoimmune disease.

Here are two questions to help you find your words:

1. What is the skill, personality trait, or characteristic that best describes what this chapter in my life taught me about myself?

Examples of -ing skills:

Building	Treasuring
Planning	Remembering
Creating	Equipping
Fixing	Laughing
Solving	Partying
Teaching	Talking
Hosting	Organizing
Listening	

Examples of traits:

Leader	Speaker
Listener	Doubter
Grower	Changer
Entertainer	Maker
Empathizer	Learner
Advocator	Show-er upper
Seeker	Retreater
Fighter	Simplifier

Examples of characteristics:

Kind	Emotionally calm
Bold	Enthusiastic
Meek	Detailed
Frugal	Patient
Generous	Zealous
Book smart/street smart	Visionary
Compassionate	

2. What is a trait or characteristic I learned about God during this season? Is it possible that the trait I saw in God was a trait God was working in me? God often gives us fruit that reflects who he is, and while it feels awkward to compare ourselves to God, we are his image bearers. I am filled with awe when I think on this: I am a dreamer because he is the ultimate dreamer. Just look at all the strange creatures out there (including me and you!). While I am an entrepreneur, he is the ultimate start-up guru, making the moon and the stars and light and dark. Can you see now how you are bearing his image and how he decided which experiences would produce fruit in you that would point back to him? He is the ultimate connection maker!

Once you've filled out your treasure map, start looking for connections, clues, similarities. Where is there similarity in experiences? What characteristics go hand in hand for a particular kind of role? For instance, when I filled out my own map, I saw words like *entrepreneur* and *teacher* several times. I saw my natural gifting in writing and articulation seep into how I became an entrepreneur. But I wouldn't have anything to write about if I didn't have kids pooping on my driveway, the blind driving, the failed dream of moving when we weren't supposed to, the student teaching debacle, and almost getting a divorce. When I wrote about it online, using my humor to make women feel understood in a deeply exhausting season and sharing my suffering in marriage, which was supposed to stop and even defeat me, it pushed me out in front of people who needed encouragement. All of a sudden, I gained influence, and through influence, I gained more ability to sell and make money. And with more money, I was able to start more businesses and further entrepreneur my little heart out—and all of it brings God's glory to my community online and in person. It's wild to see how it's all connected, and I bet your map is going to start yelling at you as you Hansel and Gretel your own way to the treasure.

The ultimate treasure is that you believe you have permission to operate audaciously and radically in your gifts, skills, and story—who you were, who you are, who you are becoming. If you believe all this to be true, everything you've just newly discovered or rediscovered about yourself frees you to live with so much purpose. And that's the best news in the universe—that God came to set the captives FREE. We aren't in slavery to who we wish we were, what talents we wish we had, what experiences have caused us suffering, and finding identity in any of it. No, we are free from all that weight. It reminds me of a time after I had my third baby when I went on my usual evening walk, feeling weird and uncomfortable in my shell of a post-baby body. Everything on my body just felt heavy. Oddly, I got this urge to run (and no one was chasing me!). I ran so hard. But when I was running, I visualized my carcass of a body falling off until I was just bones and then my bones flew to heaven and disappeared. Weird, huh?

I still think about that often. We get to run the race set before us, and not to win approval or hear an audience cheer us on, not to even prove ourselves to be good runners and in shape. We run to disappear in him so when people look at us running fully, they see him, not us. We want people to look at us and say, "What is her God like? Where is she going? How can I join?" So run hard, ladies. Run light and free. Run with wild abandonment. Run so hard you disappear and all people see is the God of goodness, the God of freedom, the God of purpose, the God of delight. Reflect the God who was. Who is. And who is to come. Live your life like it was entirely on purpose all along.

Somebody give me a hallelujah!

My Treasure Map

Write one word near each number that describes your journey through each section. They can be names of people, places, or even a code word!

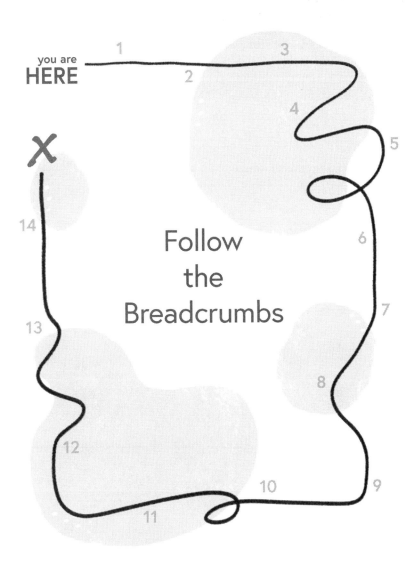

you are
HERE

1

2

3

4

5

X

6

14

Follow
the
Breadcrumbs

7

13

8

12

11

10

9

Epilogue

Here's the joke: A lady walks into a room and tells her friends she's writing a book. Everyone cheers, "Yes! You have to!" But when they get quiet, she tells them that it's going to be a memoir with a pen name because it won't fit into the Christian space all that well and it will contain cuss words.

Except it's not a joke and I have no pen name so that makes it really scary.

I joked about writing that book because I was just afraid to be myself, really me. So like I do sometimes to cover myself in protection, I used humor as a shield. So I could say, *Haha! Just kidding. I was just kidding. How hilarious was I to dream a big dream like that!* I didn't have the confidence, and I hadn't lived out some of the stories. But I am actually doing exactly what I had voiced for ten years without knowing it wasn't a silly thing I said to make people laugh. God was helping me breathe the vision into my mouth before I believed it for myself. And goodness, I sure did try to get in the way of myself many times, and crazy things blew me off my track too. Lots of loop-the-loops on this girl's map.

The truth is that I sort of wrote two books before I wrote this one. The first I wrote because I thought my marriage redemption was the only story I had to tell. Silly really, considering everyone is so layered and complicated and we often live a hundred different stories inside one grand shell of a body over our entire lives. I wanted to write it so badly. I wanted to want to write it even more. It was torturous reliving the horror of my darkest days in great detail. I know God lives in the details, but I had this ache in the back of my head: *What do all these details accomplish?* It had to be more purposeful than that. The last thing I wanted to contribute to the world was more noise. And then I started wanting to write a lot of other stories. About funny things. About complicated, family-of-origin things. About real things that show I'm a whole person, not just a lady who recovered from infidelity. The joke became less funny and more real. More tangible. I couldn't stop myself from writing honestly on the great internet, as honestly as I could at the time.

So I pitched the second book. This would be a book of stories, a memoir. There wasn't really a space for Christian women writers based solely on just telling stories with no tight religious theme. But I wanted to write about my dad riding a kid down the stairs in his robe because he caught said boy in my little sister's room the night of my other sister's wedding when the house was FULL of our relatives. I walked into the living room the next day to my dad's swollen foot propped on a chair, my mother angrily reading her Bible, my sister crying, and my memaw sleeping through it all. (Maybe my publishers will let me have a surprise chapter where I tell that story and it has no purpose except we laugh and laugh about how my dad's boxers opened while he was riding the kid and my dad's leg got tangled in the banisters and he almost got arrested because the boy's nose was broken.) But there was no point to book two, just essays of a complicated and funny life. Surprise, surprise, the book was rejected. I was disappointed, but I was also off the hook from writing a book I didn't want to write and a book that had no real point except entertainment. And then there's that funny thing about rejection. It pushes you to rethink, to reconsider, to pay attention. Rejection is how I got to the book I was supposed to write. This book.

For several months I told God, "You're the one who told me to write. You're the one who said it would happen. I've given it a college try. So you're going to have to do this because I'M OUT!" But then I found the breadcrumb.*

One day, when I was driving to the thrift store to do what I love best (buying things with stories inside them), the idea was plain as day: I would write about my marriage *and* all my complicated, sometimes funny stories, but this book would be all about giving women complete permission to see their past, present, and future as a directional compass to finding their purpose in any season. It all had a purpose, and I would be their Sherpa helping them find their own breadcrumbs!

I called my writing coach (from the first publishing house that rejected me and who kept bugging me about not giving up on writing a book) from the parking lot. "I have to write this book. I'm going to write this with or without a publisher. I know you're my coach, but consider being my agent."

"No, I don't know how to be an agent. I can help you find a great one."

"We can figure it out together. And between us we already have connections."

"I have no clue how to be an agent."

". . . and also we already work well together. . . . You seem unbothered by my antics."

"You know it's strange, but my dad always said I should be an agent."

"SEE! It's a breadcrumb!!"

We laughed. Later she would accept. God was providing for me, but he was providing for her too, weaving our stories in and out of each other's.

This time, it was right. The breadcrumbs were lining up exactly right.

....

* "If your child asks for bread, do you trick him with sawdust?" (Matthew 7:7 MSG).

183

No book is easy to write (if it is for you, you can find your medal on page 999 of this book), but this book flew out of me as Lloyd Christmas describes: "like the salmon of Capistrano." I couldn't stop finding breadcrumbs and cross-references all over my story. I was Indiana Jones searching for treasure. Along the way he gets off track, meets several friends, garners injuries, and eats some weird stuff, but he does get the treasure because he keeps looking for it and believes it's there. That's basically a good summary of my life—and yours! Life is complicated and never goes as planned, but that's the point. It's not supposed to. God has his own plans, and he lets us in on them little by little.

Along those lines, that's why we sold the lake house that we thought we would use for retreats. Like writing this book, it didn't go as planned. It became heavy and not light for us, nor did having retreats during a pandemic make sense (*womp!*). However, it was an incredible investment. We got to cash out and see God provide for us in ways we never dreamed. And I feel God stirring in me that a new idea is going to come; I can't wait to find out what that is.

Like all our stories, the book ain't over till it's over, and sometimes the bows that have wrapped up a story get untied. At this point, I've seen so many instances of God working on purpose for a purpose in my own life that I have to believe he is up to something good on my behalf, even when it's hard.

Speaking of hard, when I was writing this book during the pandemic shutdown, it felt silly to be talking about purpose when everyone was stuck at home. But it became clear that we all got a shakedown. People were deciding to quit or were forced to quit their jobs or were starting their own businesses. Many had to stay home and take care of kids and relatives and spouses. Suddenly, we all had a lot of time to think. *Is this how I really want to spend my time? Is this really what I want to do with my precious life when nothing is guaranteed?* They call it the Great Resignation. I hope as you look around at the rubble of suffering and a tumultuous political, relational, and informational climate that this book meets you with a sloppy, surprising kiss.

My heart flutters when I think about women being set free in their calling to change the world. It starts with what's right in front of us, as patronizing as it sounds. But it's not patronizing, it just feels that way because we've been patted on the heads for so long and told our greatest calling is only staying at home and having children. And while those are both worthwhile callings, there are other worthwhile callings. My Christmas wish* is that you now see the biggest permission slip written with your name on it, and it gives you permission to believe that every single event in your life is on purpose, for a purpose. Nothing about your life has been "coincidental." I hope you make your own map and cry looking at the breadcrumbs of God's goodness, his proddings, his provisions, his presence, and his callings to your heart. No self-help book you read will make you believe that unless you see it for yourself. So cheers to you holding your map, ready for the journey, full of hungry anticipation to see where God has been and where he is and where he goes before you. All in eager hope that you will actually find him.

Follow the breadcrumbs.

---

* I say this in all seasons because it makes it sound of utmost importance.

Acknowledgments

To my husband, Nato, who is named Mark, but I only call him that when I'm mad. You had more faith in me than I had in myself. I leaned on your faith often, even when I acted strong. You are the light of my life.

To my children. I know this took time away from you. Thank you for letting me live in my purpose outside mothering.

To my friends and family who had to hear about me writing a book for eight years and still kept cheering me on incessantly.

To my parents for making me who I am. I am not embarrassed of my upbringing (except Dad's socks with Jesus sandals).

To Andy for emailing me every year. "Not being annoying, just persistent. Ready to write a book?" You got the gig!

To JDL, my encouragement angel who made me feel like I MUST say the things or else the world wouldn't be the same.

To Andrea, who was my writing coach but then somehow got finagled into being my agent and also a writing coach. I would not have written this without you. And I am not being patronizing. You made me think I could write a book, and I did. Are you also a magician?

To everyone I am forgetting, you can probably find yourself in this book somewhere.

About the Author

JAMI NATO is a businesswoman, speaker, writer, and a kajillion other things. She has been married for seventeen years and manages a circus of four children while continuing to kill most plants she brings into her home. She lives in Kansas City and will argue with you if you tell her your city has the best barbecue in the nation. When not with her family, Jami power walks the trail, making friends with dogs, ducks, and anyone over seventy. To her husband's dismay, her favorite hobby is thrifting and collecting items she doesn't need, and she is passionate about beating her neighbors in cornhole.

Follow her crazy life on Instagram @jaminato or at jaminato.com.